THE TECHNIQUE
of
TELEVISION NEWS

THE LIBRARY OF COMMUNICATION TECHNIQUES

THE TECHNIQUE OF

TELEVISION NEWS

by

IVOR YORKE

Focal Press · London

Focal/Hastings House · New York

© Focal Press Limited 1978

🔖 British Library Cataloguing in Publication Data

Yorke, Ivor
    The technique of television news—(The
    library of communication techniques).
    1. Television broadcasting of news
    2. Television—Production and direction
    I. Title   II. Series
    791.45'5   PN4784.T4

ISBN (excl. USA) 0 240 51009 7
ISBN (USA only) 0 8038 7187 2

First Edition 1978

Phototypeset by Computer Photoset Limited, Birmingham
Printed in Great Britain at The Pitman Press, Bath

CONTENTS

ACKNOWLEDGEMENTS

A number of my colleagues in BBC Television News were kind enough to read the manuscript under its original working title of *Three Words A Second*, and to offer their constructive advice. I am most grateful to all of them.

In particular I should like to thank four people—John Heuston, Foreign News Editor; Bill Nicol, named News Cameraman of the Year, 1977; Michael Scarlett, now a Senior Television Engineer; and Henry Tarner, Head of Engineering, Television News. Many of the detailed suggestions they made influenced my eventual approach to certain technical matters, although the responsibility for any mistake in interpretation is, of course, my own.

I would also like to record my gratitude to all those authors and publishers who generously allowed me to make direct quotations from work in which they hold the copyright; to Autocue Products Ltd. for a photograph of one of their studio prompting devices in action; to Michael Sullivan and Robert Wheaton for the use of pictures from their personal collections; to Graham Milloy and Robin Fairweather of BBC Central Stills; to Helen Power, who deciphered an unevenly-typed, much scribbled-on final draft and transformed it into a typescript of beauty; to Alan Protheroe, Editor of *BBC Television News*, for his active encouragement as well as giving the BBC's formal permission to publish; and, finally, to my wife, Cynthia, and children Sarah and Judith, who suffered more or less in silence as normal family life, house and garden, went to rack and ruin during the three years that this book took to gestate.

Ivor Yorke,
London,
1978.

INTRODUCTION

TELEVISION is commonly a target for attack by the politicians, press and people of many countries. Some educationists see its cumulative effect as a major factor in the breakdown of respect that children are previously supposed to have had for their parents and teachers. Some moralists believe that it has contributed to sexual permissiveness, violence, vandalism and drug-taking. Television has been said to reduce the great issues of the time to trivia, to blunt the senses against man's inhumanity to man, to disrupt family life, to act as a soporific for the 'working classes', and to set back the standards of reading and writing in schools. Sneered at by its detractors as the 'goggle-box', the 'idiot tube', 'chewing gum for the eyes' and a 'vast wasteland of useless rubbish', it joins package holidays to Spain, bingo and the football pools in the pillory for being too popular by half.

Countless books have been written in an attempt to understand the phenomenon. Many have examined the political and social impact of the medium through the internationally renowned broadcasting organisations; others have dealt with its history, growth and potential. Even more have dissected television technology in general or specific terms.

In this welter of words, the documentary and current affairs broadcasts in Britain have been examined under the microscope often enough. But it is only recently that politicians, writers and sociologists have turned their attention to what is known in the trade as 'hard news'—the daily programmes which attract vast audiences for their direct, unadorned reportage of events of international, national and local importance.

Some of the criticism which has emerged echoes the tone of that made in a speech by Spiro T. Agnew,[1] whose term of office as

---

[1] Des Moines, Iowa, November, 1969.

vice-President of the United States is otherwise mostly remembered for his manner of leaving it. He once created a flutter by referring to American television newsmen as a "tiny, enclosed fraternity of privileged men elected by no one", who had a free hand in "selecting, presenting and interpreting the great issues of our nation." It has since become fashionable to suggest that a like-minded fraternity in Britain selects the news from within a narrow spectrum restricted by its members' own upbringing, education and social attitudes; that there is an unhealthy concentration on violence, gloom and doom; that (depending on the critic's own political standpoint) television news is part of a wider conspiracy either to bring about the destruction of established order and moral values or to perpetuate class divisions. And all that takes no account of the never-ending internal debate over whether television news is doing its job properly or manages only to scratch the surface of the important issues without putting them into context.

The newspaper world, meanwhile, has maintained a morbid interest in the fortunes of television and television news, developing a love–hate relationship which allows the gossip columnists in particular to dig deeply for the dirt while, simultaneously, other pages devote acres of space to programme reviews, plans and personalities in an almost sycophantic fashion. For although some journalists writing about television news display a distressing lack of knowledge of the subject, they are usually cute enough to recognise that television news *is* news. There is no disguising their glee when, as happens often enough, it has some internal strife, falls foul of higher authority, makes mistakes, shows outward signs of foolish over-spending or offends in some other way.

This attitude should come as no surprise, even to ex-newspapermen like myself, who once fondly believed that all journalists were brothers. Newspapers in general have a vested interest in seeing public confidence weaken in those to whom they lost, long ago, the title of The People's Prime Source of News. William Small of CBS News, puts it this way: "The tube is an easy target. There is a waiting audience, swelled by intellectual snobbery and professional envy, that warmly greets each new attack on television. The envy reflects television's kidnapping of exciting and powerful roles once exclusively the province of the printed press. Television in the world of reality is too important and too powerful to be left to its practitioners or its critics. It is also too complicated to be reduced to simple generalisations, critical or not."[1]

In spite of all the criticism that is made—it is tempting to say because of it—a BBC Audience Research Unit Survey[2] found a very large (though admittedly declining) percentage of consumers still considered television news the most trustworthy of all the media.

The fact remains that very few serious attempts have been made to study in detail the problems, processes and techniques involved in bringing television news to the screen several times a day, three hundred and sixty five days a year. In truth it is not an easy subject to explain. Television news cannot be easily dismissed as 'radio news with pictures' (as some broadcasting organisations attempting to set it up for themselves have discovered to their cost) or as identical to any other branch of the television business, including its first cousin, current affairs.

In his thesis on the social organisation of news production in broadcasting, the British sociologist Philip Schlesinger says the production of news "rather like the writing of history, involves the imposition of order and coherence, in brief, of meaning, upon events." Television journalists themselves would take it a stage further and say that television news is a kind of electronic jigsaw which, like other puzzles, makes no sense until it has been completed. Taking a few separate pieces at random is rather like examining the big toe and thumb and expecting them to give an accurate picture of what the whole human body looks like. In television news, the most important pieces are people, operating within their own limited spheres of influence along parallel lines which converge only at times of transmission.

How those pieces fit together may not greatly interest either the professional critics or many among the millions who make up the daily viewing audience, but it *does* concern those journalists for whom television companies all over the world are continuing to provide worthwhile and stimulating jobs at a time when there is a large question mark against the economic viability of so many newspapers.

It also concerns those employers who, fully aware of the ever-mounting pressures upon them from all sides to turn out fair, accurate programmes of a professionally high standard, need the

---

[1] William Small *To Kill A Messenger. Television News and the Real World*, (Hastings House, 1970).
[2] Annual Review of BBC Audience Research Findings, 1973–4, quoting 1970 statistics.

journalists they engage to be utterly expert and reliable. For in television news the craft of writing clearly and succinctly is only part of the battle. Much of the rest of it has to do with a bewildering battery of electronic equipment and strange technical jargon which needs to be mastered properly before a single word is written.

The journalist must also understand the nature of television itself, what he is doing, why, and how his particular role fits in with those of other members of the news team.

For these reasons the journalist, however experienced in other fields, must be suitably prepared. That means a certain amount of formal training, which is becoming vastly more important as television techniques advance and which, significantly, seems to escape more or less unscathed when economies are being demanded elsewhere.

Regrettably, even in these enlightened days of adult education, the word 'training,' so far as it applies to journalism, is one for which too many old newspaper hands still have only contempt. To them the idea that any kind of journalist can be made, rather than born, is anathema, suggesting a succession of unthinking stereotypes pouring out of the same mould. They are wrong. Training does not seek to restrict the free thinker from thinking freely about work or anything else; training in television news technique sets out to equip the recipient of it with the knowhow and confidence to employ the marvellous technical resources which are about to become tools of his or her trade.

The experienced newcomer to television news might have been employed on a weekly or daily newspaper, a news agency or radio station. The novice might have been recruited straight from university and needs initiation into journalistic fundamentals as well as the special skills required for television. The two types of recruit have one thing in common; they both need to learn, preferably as quickly as possible, *how*.

What follows in this book is not intended as a substitute for a properly run training scheme using up-to-date methods and equipment. It makes no claim to be comprehensive or set out to explain every technical nuance, especially as the terminology, methods and equipment in use are bound to vary widely. Neither does it attempt to standardise procedures for news selection and judgement. Every news team jealously guards its own, based on its status within its parent broadcasting organisation and, in turn, on the principles which guide that organisation's role under the social and political systems of the country concerned.

What this book *is* intended to be is a first reader in television news style and production technique by one working journalist for others venturing into the most exciting field of mass communication. The emphasis throughout is on what it is important for journalists or aspiring journalists to know about television news. It is an attempt to help newcomers fit the pieces of the puzzle together in as painless and non-technical a way as possible.

ELECTRONIC JIGSAW PUZZLE

How television gets its news

AMONG the inevitable first questions asked of all journalists by outsiders is "How do you get your news?" For those working in television the answer is by no means a simple one, as so much depends on the financial and technical resources each news service is able to put into its news-gathering effort. The smaller and poorer, with little to call their own, may well find themselves almost totally dependent on 'second-hand' material passed on by the sister radio services often run in parallel under the same roof, or on the international newsfilm agencies: the large, prestigious 'independents' with fat budgets are able to buy a great deal of exclusivity.

Between the two extremes, however, lies the vast amount of common territory open to world news organisations in general, whether they are engaged in putting the word out over the air waves or on the printed page.

In Britain, for example, there are the regular postal deliveries, each of which produces its share of publicity handouts sent out by government departments, public relations firms, private companies, industrial and social organisations. To this rich harvest can be added 'house' and trade magazines, official statistics, advance copies of speeches, invitations to exhibitions, trade fairs, inaugurations, openings, closings, the laying of foundation stones and other ceremonies of varying importance. Well-established fixtures—Parliamentary sessions, court sittings, state visits, sports events and anniversaries of all types—join the queue with scores of other public and semi-public events which are carefully weighed for their potential interest. Those surviving the first hurdle are noted in diaries of future events for more serious consideration nearer the day. These so-called 'diary' stories or their immediate consequences (follow-ups) probably account for the majority of news stories which appear on television and in the newspapers.

The rivals, whether they be other television or radio programmes, magazines, weekly, evening or morning papers are scoured for titbits on which to build something bigger.

Journalists working either for themselves or for other publications offer suggestions (for which they expect to be paid) on a fairly regular basis. Freelances or 'stringers' they are called, and there are whole networks of them, wooed by news editors against the day that a really major story breaks in their area. It is the stringers who provide much of the basic news. With good contacts among local police, politicians and businessmen, they are usually first on the scene of any big story in their community, and are swift to pass on the information to their larger brethren. Local or specialist news agencies, concentrating on crime reporting, sport, finance and so on, also add their contributions, but it is the large concerns in this particular field which provide most of the bread and butter written information and still photographs (some transmitted by wire) on a regular basis to the press and broadcasting organisations.

Subscribers obtain their domestic news from the British national agency, the Press Association (PA, founded 1868), owned by the chief provincial newspapers in Britain and the Irish Republic, and supplying a complete service of general, legal, Parliamentary, financial, commercial and sporting news. Exchange Telegraph (Extel, 1872), which for many years ran a parallel general service, now concentrates on financial and sporting topics. Reuters (London-based since 1851) is the main source of foreign news. It is owned by the newspapers of Britain, Australia and New Zealand through the Newspaper Publishers' Association, the Press Association, the Australian Associated Press and the New Zealand Press Association. The Associated Press (AP)—the British operating company of the Associated Press of America— and United Press International (UPI) also serve the broadcasting organisations and the Press.

The agencies themselves rely for their material on either full-time staff men or hundreds of stringers who owe first loyalty to the publications employing them. The end product of all their work can be seen every day in the hundreds of thousands of words which pour out from the tape machines clicking away in the corner of the newsroom.

This material is analogous with the raw meat fresh from the butcher. Some of the fat has been trimmed off but otherwise it is left for the customer to cook as he pleases. Television throws it to the sub-editors to be chewed, swallowed, then regurgitated into another meal more easily digested by the viewer sitting cosily at home. Newspapers treat agency copy as merely one of the ingredients from which their staff general reporters eventually produce their own masterpieces to satisfy their readers' proven tastes. These general reporters, traditionally under the wing of the news editor, are also deployed to cover the various diary items day by day, or may be detached for longer periods to work on projects and campaigns of special interest to their papers.

The television news equivalent, fewer in number than their counterparts on individual Fleet Street newspapers (from which many of them have graduated) are used mainly on the diary or follow-up assignments offering the most filmworthy possibilities. They are also engaged in spot news stories first broken by the agencies, but in either case the television news reporter has to work as part of a team. There is a cameraman to take the pictures, a recordist to capture the sound, and where interior locations are involved, a lighting assistant to supply enough artificial illumination by which the film can be exposed. Without these or other forms of technical help the reporter is powerless to produce much that is worthwhile for television. Conversely, the film crews are often briefed to cover stories without reporters, relying on their own judgements for the detailed choice of coverage. There are also one-man film units equipped with small mute cameras, but these have obvious limitations.

Other staff newspeople are specialists in particular areas of news. Regarded as experts after years of devoting themselves to a single subject and building up highly-placed personal contacts, they themselves become reliable sources for much that is important. The political editor, fresh from an off-the-record chat over lunch with a government minister; the industrial correspondent, back from talks with acquaintances influential within business, industry or the trade unions—each is ideally placed to begin piecing together information which might well develop into a big news story, perhaps not today or tomorrow, but next week.

This handful of specialist correspondents, as members of recognised groups or associations of journalists working in the same field for different news outlets, enjoy confidential 'lobby' briefings from governments and are on the regular mailing lists of professional bodies sending out material of a technical or restricted nature.

The television news organisations are also able to rely fairly heavily on their own regional structures, which are likely to employ specialist correspondents, staff and freelance reporters and camera crews. Material originated regionally can be pumped into the network news live or recorded on to videotape (see page 84) for replaying later on. In the BBC's case there are eight television newsrooms in provincial England plus others in Scotland, Wales and Northern Ireland, all of which are partly in business for the purpose of providing the national news with items deserving wider than purely local coverage, although forays by teams from London are by no means discouraged. In general, co-operation between all parties is close and continuous.[1]

In addition, the BBC controls four national radio networks centred on Broadcasting House in London, twenty local radio stations dotted about the country,[2] and Bush House, headquarters of external service broadcasts, from any of which ideas and some sound-only coverage can be picked up for use when required.[3]

Independent Television News has natural links with the 15 commercial TV programme companies operating under the umbrella of the Independent Broadcasting Authority, but it is

---

[1] BBC TV News contributes *from* London to the 25-minute regional daily news magazine programmes, sometimes calling on its own facilities and staff including the specialist correspondents, sometimes allowing network facilities to be used by regional staff brought in specially for the occasion. In all these cases the contributions may be made live or recorded at the receiving end for local transmission later. Independent Television News employs regional political correspondents who can supply copy or report directly into the regional news programmes which are considered an extremely important part of the total output of each programme company.

[2] The report of the Annan Committee into the future of broadcasting in the United Kingdom, published in March, 1977, recommended that responsibility for all local radio should be hived off from the BBC and Independent Broadcasting Authority and transferred to an entirely new Local Broadcasting Authority. The Committee was not unanimous in this view, however, one of the dissenters recognising that local stations acted as local newsgathering agencies; without this presence the BBC would either have to set up a local newsgathering organisation or see its national news output impoverished.

[3] There is also a BBC internal organisation, the General News Service, which evaluates all incoming news material from its own and news agency sources and relays a digest by teleprinter link from the central newsroom at Broadcasting House in London. A particular part of the GNS service, known as 'Rip 'n' Read,' makes complete national radio news summaries available for immediate broadcast for by local and regional BBC stations. GNS is also responsible for another internal system by which important service messages or news flashes can be broadcast to BBC London offices over a loudspeaker network. Yet another source is the Corporation's Monitoring Service, based just outside Reading, Berkshire, which passes to BBC television and radio newsrooms information culled from a round-the-clock listening service to the radio broadcasts of foreign stations—often the quickest means of obtaining international 'official' news.

almost exclusively a centralised organisation, priding itself on an ability to act swiftly in the movement of men and equipment around Britain or anywhere else in the world.

Foreign news sources

On the foreign side, some staff journalists are employed permanently away from base in any one of a small number of major centres. These, by the nature of international affairs, are the most likely to produce a stream of news stories of interest to viewers at home and, equally important, are themselves at the crossroads of the world communications systems: New York, Rome, Hong Kong, Brussels.[1]

Like his counterpart at home, the foreign specialist sees that he meets the right people, reads the local papers, watches local television, listens to local radio and gets himself accredited to local national organisations as the official representative of his television station at home. This, as a rule, will ensure a constant flow of information to be sifted for use as background material to items transmitted later on.

Though based for convenience in one place, the foreign correspondent might well have a huge territory, perhaps a whole continent, to police. This means having to cover thousands of miles to reach major stories breaking in remote areas. Time differentials frequently weigh heavily. The correspondent may have to work through the night to produce the goods for bosses for whom it is still day. He will probably wear two watches, one keeping local time, the other 'home' time to remind him constantly of deadlines.

With skill and good fortune, the foreign correspondent will become an accepted part of the local scenery, sometimes as an honoured guest. Elsewhere, there may be hostility thinly disguised as toleration. The correspondent's home is bugged, the telephone tapped. He and his wife are followed. Eventually, he commits what the government of the country regards as a professional indiscretion and is expelled.

Where full-time television newsmen are not based, the foreign

---

[1] The news value of each base is kept under continuing close scrutiny and changes are made to keep pace with the emergence of new areas of special interest. The most recent movement has tended to be away from western Europe towards southern Africa, which is considered likely to produce major stories until well into the eighties. At the same time there has been a significant improvement in the region's communications with the opening of the South African television service and the building of a satellite ground station near Johannesburg.

equivalent of the home stringer is frequently employed. Sometimes this is a local national serving any number of overseas outlets. Often, he is a foreigner himself. He may be a freelance accepting occasional commissions outside his normal field, or a staff correspondent of one publication which, in an effort to keep down the very considerable costs involved in maintaining a presence abroad, allows him to pass material to others. In addition to all these permutations, in the case of the BBC there are also staff working abroad for radio, and these can be borrowed by the television side when the occasion arises.

In some foreign centres the television news man has easy access to locally-based film or electronic camera units who are hired for a daily fee when required. In one or two particularly busy areas for news, camera crews are employed on semi-permanent contracts. Their film is usually shipped home by air for developing, editing and transmission, although there are occasions when the nature and immediacy of the material dictates that it is handled locally, using hired laboratory and editing staff and then transmitted direct through the Eurovision network or by the use of communications satellites. (See pages 148–152.) This speedy system, which saves many hours, is being used more and more widely by the international newsfilm agencies which supply foreign news to hundreds of television news programmes throughout the world. Their links with the major networks give them immediate access to a staggering choice of first-class news material, and they also employ their own staff and freelance camera crews in important centres.

For the poorer countries not able to send their own staff, agency coverage is relatively cheap and is usually perfectly adequate in terms of coverage quality, whether broadcast in its entirety complete with sub-titles to augment the foreign language commentary, or reduced in length and transmitted alongside a locally-written script from the paperwork accompanying every film.

The bulk of this material is provided by the big three international newsfilm agencies. Visnews, beginning life in 1957 as the British Commonwealth and International Newsfilm Agency, is owned jointly by the BBC, Reuters and several Commonwealth broadcasting organisations. It numbers the BBC among its chief subscribers in more than eighty countries. UPITN was formed in 1967 as a partnership between the television department of United Press International and Independent Television News.

The result is a worldwide network of staff and stringer cameramen who shoot film and move it to the nearest point for transmission to both ITN and clients in other countries. CBS News, part of the wealthy American network organisation, started its syndication service in 1953.

Between them, these agencies now provide well over half the visual material available to member organisations involved in the Eurovision News Exchange network. Much of it has the merit of being the first film of a major event, to which the wealthier TV news organisations may decide to despatch their own staff units later on. Even when they do, the agencies are relied upon to continue their coverage for the rest of their clientele.

The agencies are also an important source of historical or background material for news programmes. Potted biographies, film and still photographs of events and places previously or likely to be in the news are rapidly made available when occasion demands, even though the material may consist of no more than a single, portrait-type photograph of an obscure politician, or a few seconds of film.

Most TV news departments also maintain their own archives, largely built up from material they have already transmitted. In some cases the 'library' is run by a film editor as part of normal duties and consists of a few cans of film kept on the cutting room shelf plus a drawer of 35mm colour slides. At best, others have expanded to become sophisticated storehouses of stills, film and videotape. These represent hundreds of thousands of separate news items, each carefully catalogued and indexed by trained full-time staff to ensure that the ultimate user has accurate and immediate access. The storage of this mass of bulky material in itself provides an enormous headache, and the regular pruning necessary demands thoroughness without carelessness. This is no mean task when there is constant pressure to make room for new additions.

Vast libraries of press cuttings and previously broadcast news scripts are also collected under the supervision of qualified staff. With literally millions of pieces of paper involved, the problem here again is the obvious one of storage space, and one solution has been to transfer older cuttings to microfilm.

To this wide and fascinating mix of home grown and expensively garnered news material can be added an unexpected occasional bonus—the 'tip-off' from a member of the public, or the amateur with a holiday snap or 8mm home movie film which

21

turns out to be a genuine exclusive for the organisation lucky enough to get it.

Who does what in television news?

If television news is a jigsaw puzzle, then most of the pieces represent highly skilled technicians with special contributions to make towards building up the final picture. For, in modern industrial jargon television is 'labour intensive', which, in other words, means that a large percentage of what it costs to run such an organisation is spent on the wages bill. Value for money is therefore essential.

Purely local broadcasting, frequently run on a shoestring budget, demands nothing if not versatility from its people. In its mildest form this may mean an engineer operating a television camera one day and a videotape recording machine the next, or all journalists reading as well as writing their own material. In extremes, this versatility requires the journalists physically to edit film as part of a normal day's work, and cameramen to write commentaries to some of the pictures they have taken.

Neither do national news organisations escape the need to make economies. One senior news editor in the Caribbean spends the first two-thirds of the day as a news-gatherer and writer for the network programme and the other third as technical director.

In the mid-seventies, a west European television news service was still operating without any permanent journalistic staff at all, apart from the chief editor. The writing for the main evening bulletins was undertaken by journalists who had already completed a full day's work elsewhere. Even among the more fortunate it is not uncommon for television news to have to share such basic services as film crews, film editors, equipment and transport with sister departments within the same organisation, even though obvious problems arise from the need to serve more than one master.

At the other end of the scale, for example, in the BBC, the television news department within the organisation is self-supporting, inasmuch as it has the exclusive use of its own separate staff, studios and technical equipment in a specially built wing of the Television Centre in West London, while remaining part of a public corporation responsible for a vast range of television and radio output. Independent Television News, which shares a building with UPITN in Wells Street, central London, is a non-profit making company owned and financed by the 15 British independent programme contractors and charged under the Television Act with the responsibility of producing national news programmes for the country's commercial network.

Chiefly because of the demands made on them to produce programmes at least twice or three times a day every week, these and other 'big league' members each need full-time staffs totalling several hundred, divided into smaller groups of specialists—reporters, film editors, studio directors, graphic artists, newsroom journalists, newsreaders, etc., who rarely, if ever, stray from their own clearly defined duties.

These sections may then be arranged into two broad categories. One is responsible for *gathering* the news (*intake* or *input*), the other for its *selection* and final shape on the screen (*output*). The linchpin of the whole structure is what is known as the 'editor-for-the-day' system. This gives to one very experienced journalist at a time operational control over one day's entire news coverage, treatment and output. The main benefit is seen as the continuity it provides, for each editor's spell on duty may be twelve hours or more, covering the transmission of several news bulletins. This is in direct contrast to the system which puts a single programme under the control of the same person every day.

Each editor is supervised from a distance by the senior executives who head the news department and are ultimately responsible

---

This is how a typical news service might be split:

———EDITOR FOR THE DAY———

INTAKE	OUTPUT
News organisers	Newsroom editorial staff
Forward planners	Film editors
Reporters	Film library
Correspondents	Production and studio staff
Film operations organisers	Telecine engineers
Film crews	Graphics and stills departments
Sound recording engineers	Newsreaders
ENG and	
Outside broadcast units	
Processing laboratory	
technicians	
Foreign news	

for its overall performance. But at an operational level the daily chain of command extends from the editor for the day to all the departments which provide their individual skills to order.

The role of intake

Aside from his operational duties on the day, the editor also has to shoulder a large degree of responsibility for anticipating what will appear on the screen. Lengthy planning meetings are held daily, weekly and monthly, at which the meticulously-compiled diaries are considered event by event under the guidance of the domestic and foreign news specialists whose job it is to deal with the logistics of news coverage.

At this stage the editor is really gazing into the crystal ball, trying to foretell what the news programmes on his next duty day will, in part, contain even though it is clearly understood by all concerned that the most expensive, carefully-laid plans will be scrapped at the last moment should a really important story break unexpectedly. It is a hazard readily accepted by everyone, not least by those who may have spent many hours 'setting up' interviews or obtaining permission to film news items which may never be seen.

Such flexibility is a routine but essential part of the news-gathering process, which is relatively slow under even the most favourable conditions. It has long been recognised that coverage for factual television programmes has to be organised well in advance to ensure that people and equipment are properly pos-itioned as an event takes place. To that extent it is far simpler to call off coverage than it is to lay it on.

The major responsibility for either eventuality rests with the duty *news organiser* or *news editor*, as the mainstay of that part of intake dealing with domestic subjects (which invariably account for the greater proportion of air time than foreign news items). With these journalists, through the day's editor and the depart-ment heads, rest the moment-to-moment decisions of when to send staff reporters and camera crews on assignments or when to call on regional or freelance effort to produce the goods. The news organisers often see themselves, somewhat cynically, as the 'can-carriers' of news departments. They are meant to have the mental agility of chess grand-masters in moving pieces (in this case reporters and camera units) into position before events occur, at the same time making sure that enough human resources remain

24

available in reserve to deal with any important new events which may arise.

The work also demands a certain intuition about the workings of senior colleagues' minds. In briefing reporters, for example, organisers are expected to know instinctively how any one editor would want an assignment carried out, down to the detail of questions to be asked in interviews.

The role of the news organiser/editor is generally restricted to arranging on-the-day coverage, much of which is based on plans previously laid by other members of the department. The duties of these *news planners* include the submission of ideas for, and the treatment of, the various items. But the routine calls chiefly for a well-developed news sense. This must be keen enough to isolate from an embarrassing wealth of incoming information about subjects for potential coverage, that tiny proportion which has some small chance of reaching the screen.

Much of the planners' time is spent making telephone calls to verify whether what seems interesting on paper will actually stand up to the closer scrutiny of a film or electronic camera, and whether the various ingredients, as discussed, are likely to result in a clear and balanced report eventually being transmitted. Once the broad details have been agreed, each item, now formalised under a one or two-word code name, is added to the internally circulated list of subjects for prospective coverage. At a still later stage, arrangements may have to be made to collect any documents or special passes needed on the day, so that the process of physically gathering the news may be carried out as smoothly as possible.

Working in close harmony with the news organisers and planners are the staff concerned with the technical side of intake. An executive variously named *film operations organiser*, *assignments editor/manager* or *film unit manager* allots the film crews and lighting assistants their stories, with or without reporters, probably keeping in touch by means of two-way radio telephones installed at base and in the camera cars. Electronic camera units may come under the same supervision, although, as one of the quirks of the system, these may be manned largely by output staff. (See pages 31–32).

The big, sophisticated intakes also employ clerical staff whose duties include booking telecommunication cable links for the transmission of material originating from regional and other outside sources, plus a small posse of motor-cyclists who play an indispensable part in the collection of urgent material.

Foreign news is also usually considered part of intake, its small presence at head office the tip of a formidable iceberg made up of staff correspondents resident abroad, a world-wide network of stringers, and close ties with friendly broadcasting organisations able to conjure words and pictures from virtually anywhere in the globe at very short notice. The department is headed by a *foreign news editor*. He is invariably a senior journalist whose professional interests are expected to extend beyond the boundaries of his own organisation into the multi-national 'clubs' specifically established to provide regular, free-flowing exchanges of news material between member countries. On a formal basis the foreign editors of BBC TV News and ITN take their turns to act as co-ordinators for the European club—the European Broadcasting Union's Eurovision News Exchange. It is a ten-day task occurring twice a year, and involves acting as chairman/referee of the daily conference hook-up at which offers of coverage are made or requested, all of which is achieved without the need for anyone to leave his office.

The routine administrative load is shared by *deputy* or *assistant foreign editors*, while operationally the better-off can afford to man the foreign desk with two or three *foreign duty editors* working in rotation. These are the equivalent of the news organisers on the domestic side, providing a link between the news-gatherers in the field and the programme editors. The despatch of home-based staff on 'fire-brigade' assignments is a matter for negotiation between the more senior members of the department.

The last link in the foreign chain is the *foreign traffic manager*, who makes the detailed arrangements for the collection of film and electronically transmitted material and who needs to be in frequent direct contact with other broadcasting organisations, particularly during the regular morning conference between Eurovision members.

The three faces of output

As a far bigger, more complicated operation than news-gathering, television news output relies on the resources provided by three separate services functioning under the loose headings of editorial, production and technical. Among the craftspeople who work in these three groups lies the same sort of generally friendly rivalry which exists between a newspaper's journalists and printers. But all are acutely aware of the fact that, however expert in their own field, no one group alone is capable of taking the material produced by intake and putting it on the screen.

Decision-making begins and ends with the editor of the day who, as the senior member of the editorial team, usually bases himself in the newsroom, where communications with the rest of output and intake are most easily maintained. According to personal whim, each editor exerts a different amount of influence to ensure that his programme follows its intended course. But with so many calls upon his time and so many loose ends to be tied during an often frantically busy duty period, the actual fighting of the battle tends to be led by a senior lieutenant, the *chief sub-editor*,[1] whose function is very similar to that of his newspaper counterpart.

The chief's responsibilities are defined most simply as those of quality controller and time-keeper. Quality control begins with the briefing of the newsroom writing staff, perhaps six or eight people, who are preparing the individual elements within the programme framework. It continues with the checking of every written item as completed, so that all the strands knit together in a way which maintains continuity while avoiding repetition, and that standards of style and grammar are kept on an even keel throughout the programme. This may mean striking out or altering phrases, perhaps even re-writing whole items composed in haste by people working under intense pressure. Also, as a journalist of great experience, the chief sub-editor has further value as a kind of editorial long-stop, preventing factual errors creeping through in a way which would ultimately damage the credibility of the entire programme.

Since there are few if any regularly open-ended news programmes the chief sub-editor's talents are meant to include a facility for speedy and accurate mental arithmetic, essential for his other role as time-keeper. Steering a whole programme towards its strict time allocation is no mean feat, especially as so much depends on intuition or sheer guesswork about the duration of segments which may not be completed until the programme is already on the air.

For this reason the chief continually has to exhort those entrusted with individual items to restrict themselves to the 'space' they have been allotted. A typical half-hour news programme may contain twelve or more separate stories varying in importance

[1]As used by ITN. BBC TV and Radio news gives identical responsibilities under the term Senior Duty Editor (SDE).

and length. An unexpected, additional ten or fifteen seconds on each would play havoc with all previous calculations, resulting in wholesale cuts and alterations. These, in turn, would probably ruin any attempts to produce a balanced, well-rounded programme.

A further stage in the chief sub's time-keeping duties comes during transmission itself, when the appearance of late news may call for what newspaper men know as 'cutting on the stone'. In the case of television this is the deletion of material to ensure that, whatever changes have to be made, a programme does not over-run its allocation of air-time, even by as little as a few seconds.

Newspaper terminology has also been borrowed to name another role in the newsroom's output operation—that of *copytaster*. In broadcasting this is not always considered a particularly senior position. The copytaster's duties are largely confined to keeping individual writers fuelled with news agency tape about the stories already chosen for inclusion by the editor.

The journalist newcomer to television news is more than likely to join the newsroom's pool of writing staff, usually the largest single group employed on the editorial side of output. Although (depending on individual organisation) they may be known as *sub-editors*, *news editors*, *scriptwriters*, *news-writers* or simply *writers*, the tasks they are called upon to perform are bound to be broadly similar.[1]

Within the limits of responsibility as defined by their senior colleagues, the news-writers assemble the components which make up every programme item, selecting still photographs, artwork, film, videotape, writing commentaries and liaising with contributing reporters and correspondents.

The most senior are often put in charge of small teams of other writers to make miniature productions out of particularly complex news items comprising different elements. The most junior, supervised carefully by the chief sub-editor or another parent-figure, may contribute only a few seconds of air-time from a pile of news agency copy. Some writers go on to develop other techniques of television and, as a result, are occasionally called upon to display their talents as producers, directors or reporters on the screen.

---

[1] In BBC regional offices the newsroom journalists also have definite intake responsibilities. They do much of the detailed research work, brief reporters and cameramen, and are also in direct contact with the network news headquarters when contributions to national programmes are being made.

As the journalistic backbone of output, linking production and technical staff with the news-gatherers of intake, the news-writers exert considerable influence over what the public eventually sees on the screen. (See pages 36–39).

Production as part of output

Even though the use of small electronic cameras for the gathering of pictorial news is gaining popularity, most of the world's television news programmes are sure to be dependent for some time yet on the raw material of 16mm sound colour film. That, in turn, means dependence on a highly-skilled staff capable of handling celluloid at a speed suitable for news work.

As with any photographic material, the first stage for exposed newsfilm is to take it from the camera to a chemical development process. Some film arrives already developed (usually from the newsfilm agencies) and some organisations employ outside laboratories to do it for them. But the *processors* working for units with their own equipment find themselves putting several thousand feet of film through the 'soup' (processing plant) every day of the week.

All developed film ultimately reaches the *film editors*, who work closely with writers from the newsroom to view, cut and assemble the material into coherent story lines within lengths dictated by the programme editor. Edited news film stories may run to a few seconds or several minutes according to importance. As with the editorial side of output the senior, more experienced practitioners are given the more complicated items to put together. The junior staff handle those involving simple cutting of minor stories (which may not even get on the air) and material copied from the archives.

Dubbing mixers, drawing on libraries of sound effects recorded on disc recordings or magnetic tape, add extra sound tracks to synchronise with the edited pictures. *Make-up editors* are responsible for physically joining completed films and sound tracks into the correct sequence for transmission. *Telecine engineers* load the reels of film into their telecine machines, devices for the electronic transmission of film which, in effect, combine the functions of television cameras and projectors.

Other production staff are closely concerned with the operation of the studio control room, the central point through which all programme sources are routed.

The main occupants of the studio itself are the *newsreaders* or *newscasters*, the public faces of the programme, on whom the success or failure of any news service may be said to depend. Although reading other people's written work aloud for limited periods each day may not seem either particularly onerous or intellectually demanding, consistently high standards of news-reading are not easily reached, and there are other pressures to offset the undoubted glamour of the job.

Unseen by the viewer, other studio staff have their own tasks to perform—the *prompter operator*, tucked away in a corner at the controls of a machine which enables the newsreader to speak the script apparently from memory; *television cameramen*, operating the three or four electronic cameras providing the pictures; and the *floor manager*, supervising the whole studio operation and using a headphone-microphone set to stay in touch with colleagues sitting facing a bank of preview monitors in the control room on the other side of the studio's glass wall.

Although the technical responsibility for every programme rests with a senior *engineer*, the creative head of the control room on transmission is the *studio director*, sometimes known as a *production assistant* (*PA*), who co-ordinates all the resources offered by the three areas of output. Helping to fuse these together at the critical moment is a *production secretary*[1] to control the exact timing of different elements, a *vision mixer* to press buttons on a console introducing the visual selections as made by the PA, and a *sound mixer* to bring in the accompanying sounds from microphones, tapes, records, film sound tracks, etc. Slight errors or delays in reaction by any member of this team are instantly translated into noticeable flaws on the screen.

Two other creative groups come within the category of production:

Graphic artists are engaged full-time on the provision, in accepted 'house' style, of all artwork used in television news—maps, charts, diagrams and lettering for the captions identifying people on the screen;

Stills assistants, research and maintain a permanent, expanding library of photographic prints and slides, some of which are taken by staff *photographers*, assigned to supplement material provided by freelances and the international agencies.

---

[1] News Transmission Assistant (NTA) in BBC News.

Technical output

Distinctions between production and technical faces of output are frequently extremely thin, since both demand many common skills. This is perhaps most noticeable in the case of *videotape editors*, who have both output *and* intake responsibilities, and are expected to combine technical mastery over highly-sensitive electronic recording machines with a film editor's awareness of the editorial values of pictures and sound. The ability to reach this state has lifted much videotape editing for news to heights at which the assembly of very complex items, particularly from foreign sources, is achieved with remarkable accuracy and speed. On a daily basis, the technical staff are directly responsible to a senior colleague from the engineering department for the maintenance and operation of equipment. Their first aim is to maintain the highest possible technical standards but at the same time to remain flexible in outlook, for compromise is necessary where picture and sound material may be low in quality but regarded as high in news value. Engineering tasks, though rarely sharing the limelight, are nevertheless central to the existence of any programme. Without them the carefully-constructed jigsaw puzzle of television news would fall apart.

News OB unit and electronic news gathering

Engineering staff also provide the main manpower for one or any number of News *OB* (outside broadcast) *units*, scaled-down versions of the multi-electronic camera teams supplying large scale picture and sound coverage, often live, of major 'set-piece' events.

A standard four or five camera OB unit covering a football match might consist of perhaps thirty people and at least three vehicles, each about 35 ft (10,668 mm) in length, making deployment difficult in all except the most carefully planned circumstances. A news OB, responding through intake to matters of immediate concern, might have to manage with up to six technicians, a single member of the production staff (a director), two cameras and two medium-sized vans, one acting as a mobile control centre.

Once in position, news OBs are ideal for coping with late-breaking events where the film camera-processing-editing formula would be too slow. But, small though it may be, each unit takes up to an hour to rig (set up) from time of arrival on location.

31

There is an electrical power source to be found, a collapsible dish-shaped aerial to be erected on high to relay the picture back to base for direct or recorded transmission, and the heavy cameras to be manoeuvred into place, connected by cable to one of the vans.

Still smaller news OBs, packing everything into a field car, are also active, but even they lack the mobility and versatility of another system which has already given some television news services a glimpse of the future. This is *ENG*, electronic news gathering, (also known as EJ, Electronic Journalism or ECC, Electronic Camera Coverage) a self-contained, miniaturised unit operated by two people equipped with a light, high quality television camera powered by a pack of batteries strapped to the cameraman's back. The camera output can be used in any one of three ways: first, for direct broadcast; second, for recording on to the unit's own small videotape machine; third, for transmission back to base, where the incoming pictures can be recorded for news staff to make their decisions about editing. The sequences are then assembled for transmission on highly-accurate editing machines.

In the United States in particular, ENG is already beginning to be regarded by some television stations as a complete substitute for film. KMOX-TV in St. Louis, Missouri, have demonstrated their faith in the new system by replacing all film cameras, processing, viewing and editing facilities at one fell swoop. They seem well pleased with the result. The otherwise 'dead' time needed for conventional film processing is now utilised far more profitably by ENG units staying on location, and the entire operation seems to be altogether faster, cheaper, more efficient and, perhaps even more important, the station's audience ratings have improved, too.[1]

An increasing number of major news events in the US are being covered by ENG crews. Television reporting of the 1976 Party Conventions and United States Presidential election was dominated by these mobile electronic units. Japanese coverage of the London economic summit of May 1977 included ENG pictures which were beamed home by satellite and, as a bonus, also transmitted by the BBC as part of their domestic news output. Five months later, on October 10, the BBC's own ENG era opened when, as the first assignment in a 12-month experi-

[1]For a fuller account of the introduction of ENG in St. Louis see *Television*, journal of the Royal Television Society, Vol. 16 No. 3. May–June, 1976.

ment, an interview with Mrs Margaret Thatcher, the Conservative Party Leader, was recorded at the House of Commons and shown on the mid-day news programme.

By 1980 the CBS network plans to have more than seventy ENG units in operation, and the time is fast approaching when, at least in the United States, it will be difficult to find laboratories able to process newsfilm. Nevertheless, news services introducing the new technology are, for the most part, likely to tread fairly warily, retaining some film capacity indefinitely, but there seems little doubt that the whole business of gathering news is in the throes of radical change.

INTRODUCING THE NEWS WRITER

Writing for television news

THE first thing to be said to the apprehensive newcomer about writing for television news is that there are any number of broad guidelines to be followed but very few hard and fast rules. This makes sound commonsense in a medium where so much depends on instant reaction in the field or in the newsroom, up to the moment of transmission.

The television news department of the British Broadcasting Corporation, the pioneers of illustrated news on British television, has no formal style book. In 1976, more than twenty years after its creation, a new editor of BBC News launched a brief, much-publicised blitz on what he considered to be the sloppy use of language which had crept in to the daily programmes. On a more regular basis, a growing newsroom log tries to signpost any editorial pitfalls as they present themselves, and there exist certain established 'house' styles in the area of type-faces, colours and formats of news artwork. But the *writers* are otherwise free of the straitjacket into which much newspaper material is forced by the tyranny of the style book.

On my very first morning as a trainee reporter with a London suburban weekly, I was given a fifty or sixty page hard-cover volume to treat with the same reverence as I would the Bible. It told me that, among other things, I was always to spell the word organ*ize* rather than organ*ise*, that the title *Councillor* had to be abbreviated to *Cllr.*, *Alderman* to *Ald.*, that it was not the *High Rd.*, or even the *High Road* but the *High-road*, and so on. In later years, I worked in a newspaper office where the length of each paragraph had to be one sentence . . . in another office, *two*. These sentences, it was made clear, must not begin with the definite or indefinite article, or with the word *But*, and that it was a journalistic crime, punishable by ridicule, to refer to the *18-year-old* defendant in a court case when, all along, we really meant the *18 years old* one.

34

All that may seem very trivial, and in many ways indeed it is. But the fact remains that so far as the printed page is concerned, uniformity and consistency within the columns are considered more likely to please the reader than to repel.

Haphazard changes of type face or different spellings of the same word are guaranteed to irritate and annoy, and experts in design are much sought after to bring discipline and order to newspaper pages so that the reader's eye may be led smoothly from one item to another.

By its nature, television news cannot expect to do precisely the same. While it is certainly both desirable and possible to lead the viewer from event to event by the proper employment of visual signposts combined with careful phraseology, what occurs within the brief time-scale of many a broadcast news item is open to each viewer's personal interpretation of what is being seen and heard.

It is this extra dimension which helps to place television in its unique position among methods of communication. A newspaper's verbatim report of a major political speech, will give a clear record of what is said; a newspaper reporter's word picture will give, at one remove, an interpretation of what is meant. A direct radio broadcast will enable what is said to be heard complete with repetitions, hesitations and 'bad' grammar. But only the television viewer, sitting in the comfort of his own home, is given the full information from which to make a personal assessment of the *way* things are said—together with the sidelong glance and nervous twitch which accompanies the confident-sounding delivery.

Unfortunately, it is extremely probable that the viewer will be shown a relatively small sample on which to base that judgement, as it is freely admitted by television newspeople that the 'whole' story, however important, can rarely, if ever, be told within the context of a routine twenty-five or thirty-minute news programme sandwiched between the domestic comedy show and the detective story. Even if there were no pictures and the newsreader read continuously for an entire half-hour, it would not be possible to pack in more than about five and a half thousand words—fewer than the front page of the London *Times*.

However long they might like to linger over recounting events of the day, television news journalists are acutely conscious that, through no fault of their own, they have to be ultra-selective, both in the number of items put on the screen and the amount of time devoted to each. Critics outside and inside television news are convinced that these factors in themselves result in restrictions on the type of material which can be included, and that a direct comparison shows the remarkable similarity between the content and treatment of news transmitted by the two national broadcasting organisations in Britain.

Whether or not this is entirely true, there is little doubt that the time element does impose an important form of constraint on the newsroom-based journalist in particular. Yet whether it has only negative influence is arguable. The need to condense forces continuing re-assessment of the merits of individual items as they develop, ensures economy in the use of words, and discourages length for its own sake. Above all, it sharpens the newsman's traditional ability to recognise those facts which cry out for inclusion from those which do not.

Application of this news-sense is, however, only one half of the newsroom journalist's function. The other half, probably more important, is to put across the chosen facts in a way that every television viewer can readily understand. It does not mean pandering to the lowest common denominator of intelligence, but it does pose a problem which does not apply to the printed word.

The British newspaper reader fed with a regular diet of the *Daily Mirror*, for example, soon learns to expect every issue to be treated in the same bright and breezy style with which he has become familiar. The regular subscriber to *The Times* will come to expect the treatment to be sober and more discursive. Television news has to satisfy *both* at the same time.

Helping the writer to do that is a powerful double-edged weapon—the capacity to let the viewer see and hear events for himself. That advantage must not be squandered, either by the use of technical resources for their own sake (so complicating otherwise uncomplicated issues) or by the presentation of written material in a way which appeals to only one half of the intellectual spectrum. Ed Murrow, one of the most outstanding of all broadcasting journalists, recognised that fact long ago when he told CBS radio reporters to use language which would be understood by the truck driver yet not insult the professor's intelligence.

Today's sophisticated audience has become accustomed to hearing everyday words and phrases used in films, the theatre, and on television. The news is no exception. It must be *told* in an authoritative, yet friendly and informal way which attracts and maintains interest without going as far as page three of Rupert Murdoch's *Sun*. Even though the total audience may add up to millions, the writer should be encouraged to think *small*, perhaps imagining people in groups of two or three. Conversational language (not slang) preferably used in short sentences, should be the aim. The point which even experienced television journalists keep in the front of their minds is that their efforts will be totally wasted if the viewer does not immediately grasp the sense of what is being said, particularly when film or some other illustration is competing with the spoken word. The admission may be painful to journalists, but the old cliché that one picture is worth a thousand words has more than a ring of truth.

The newspaper reader can always return to the printed sentence. If necessary he can pore over a dictionary. But words once uttered on television (or radio, of course), are beyond recall. A viewer left wondering about the meaning of what has been said at the beginning of a sentence will probably be too distracted to comprehend what is being said at the end of it. That applies to every television news item, without exception, and almost the greatest crime that any journalist in the medium can commit is to leave any part of the audience in confusion about what is meant. The onus is on the writer, always, to put across the spoken word in as clear, simple and direct way as possible.

Of course it is far simpler to create this principle than it is to carry it through, especially where some government publications, wordy official announcements or complicated economic and industrial subjects are concerned. Perhaps the writer is then left with a single, overriding test—does *he* understand what he is writing? If not, neither will the viewer.

The fact remains that the successful news script probably has as much to do with proper mental preparation as it has with an ability to put words together in a clear way.[1] The journalist working in television must be already tuned in to the task ahead before anything is written. Watching yesterday's programme, listening to this morning's radio news bulletins, reading the national newspapers every day, may at times be regarded as chores to be avoided, but the journalist who is not well-informed

---

[1] Some very old hands maintain that the best scripts are dictated without being put on paper initially, so ensuring the use of spoken language. If that seems too difficult, a compromise is to assimilate as much information as possible from agency tape or other sources, write a draft script and re-check the source material later to confirm detail. The result should then be read aloud to test its suitability for speech.

and up to date on a wide range of current subjects is unlikely to be genuinely authoritative when it comes to informing others. The sacrifice of 'pleasure' reading time for 'duty' reading time is an unavoidable necessity of professional life. That each journalist should be keenly aware of what is going on in the world will appear to be stating the obvious: it is a matter for regret that an astonishing number are ill-informed, and proud of it.

There is also a proper routine to be observed once the writer is given the day's assignments in the newsroom. Where applicable, there are the relevant newspaper cuttings, reference books and pamphlets to be consulted, coverage details to be discussed with correspondents contributing from abroad or with reporters conducting interviews, changes of emphasis to be watched in 'running' stories. Where film is concerned, a close check needs to be kept on progress from location to processing department to cutting room. In other words, unlike the newspaper sub-editor, whose role is similar but not the same, the television news-writer does not simply sit still and wait for things to occur. By the time the moment comes to put words on paper the journalist should be in complete control of the shape and content of that part of the programme for which he is responsible.

Equally important is every writer's recognition that his own contributions, however important, represent only one fraction of the broadcast. There must be conscious awareness of the preceding and following items in the order of transmission so that, where appropriate, the right phrases may be used to smooth the transition from one subject to the next.

Knowledge of what is in the rest of the programme ought to be automatic, but it is not. Editorial staff often admit that they are so engrossed in their own particular duties that they are totally unaware of what their colleagues around them are doing. It is a standing joke that the day will come when a sub-editor handling down-bulletin pictures of a VIP opening some prestige project will be working away in a cutting room, blissfully ignorant of the fact that, on his way back to the office, that same VIP has been run over by a passing steamroller or blown up by a terrorist bomb.

Three words a second

Finally, although both the television and newspaper journalist trade in words, what ultimately distinguishes one from the other may be seen as a matter of arithmetic.

The newspaper sub-editor calculates in *space*—ems, ens,

points and column inches. The television writer works in *time*—minutes and seconds, and the formula that three words of English take one second for a professional to read aloud on the air provides the fundamental basis of all news writing for television. This takes into account not only the slight variations in pace between readers but also the different lengths of words used in normal, spoken language. It has, despite the scepticism of successive generations of newcomers to television news-writing, proved itself remarkably accurate, and it is equally adaptable to other languages when calculated in syllables rather than whole words.

Building up the story

The most simple method of telling the news on television is for the newsreader to read the writer's words direct to the viewer through the television camera and the microphone in the studio. In the terminology of television, the newsreader becomes *on camera* (*On Cam.*) In BBC TV News the reader is said to be *in vision*, which makes the written item itself a *vision story*.

All television news programmes contain varying numbers of vision stories, most of which are the products of heavily edited news agency tape. Sometimes they are complete in themselves. More often they are used as a base from which the newsreader launches some visual material, hence the frequent use of the term *vision intro*. Theoretically, although a vision story may be of any duration, editors of news programmes have a tendency to keep lengths down within reasonable limits for fear that the programme presentation as a whole may seem to lack pace and variety. It is also felt that long vision stories, those going much beyond a minute (180 words), do not make the fullest use of television's possibilities. Conversely, there is believed to be little point in producing a vision story shorter than two sentences. Anything less seems unlikely to register with the viewer.

Superficially, there may appear to be very little difference between the vision story, the newspaper article or even the piece of agency tape torn from the teleprinter. In fact there are essential variations. The opening paragraph of any newspaper item will make a point of establishing four main facts—who, what, where and when, as in the typical example:

Luton, Bedfordshire, Thursday.
Three men armed with shot-guns forced their way into the

High-street branch of Pitkin's Bank here this afternoon and held staff and customers hostage for nearly an hour while two other members of the gang stripped the vault of an estimated £75,000 in cash and jewellery from safe-deposit boxes . . .

An attempt to follow precisely the same pattern on television, with so many facts packed into a very short space would almost inevitably lead to confusion in the viewer's mind.

Shuffling the identical details into a different order, the television newswriter should attempt to explain the incident in much the same kind of simple, easy manner he would use to a group of friends:

There's been a big bank raid at Luton, about thirty miles from London. An armed gang held customers and staff hostage for nearly an hour before making off with cash and jewellery worth about seventy five thousand pounds. The bank, a branch of Pitkin's . . .

Using the same technique, even such complicated, essential subjects as the monthly Trade Figures or Retail Price Index need hold no terrors for the writer, although both statistics may arrive for publication at the same time:

The economy's continuing to show signs of improvement, according to two new sets of official figures. For the sixth month running Britain sold more abroad than ever before, and prices in the shops have also dropped again.

Once that basic message has been put across, the i's can be dotted and the t's crossed with diagrams prepared by the graphics department.

But it is accepted that opening sentences do represent one of the most difficult areas for writers seeking a compromise between impact and full comprehension. There is, for example, nothing much wrong with this sentence:

Railway fares are going up by ten per cent on most routes from the Autumn.

yet if heard with anything less than full attention at least one of the four facts may be missed. The alternative leaves little margin for error. First, the viewer is hooked:

Railway fares are going up again

then firmly landed:

The increases, averaging ten pence in the pound on most routes, take effect in the Autumn.

Of course there are occasions when this approach would be considered far too soft and tentative. The television newswriter must then talk in bold headlines:

Three hundred people have been killed in the world's worst air crash.

The Government has been defeated in the Commons.

President Nixon has resigned.

The transition from these to less momentous events is sometimes achieved best by the use of a form of words, most easily described as a *side heading*, to signify change of pace and subject:

Next, the economy.

At home . . .

In the Middle East . . .

Now sport.

The phrases themselves are perhaps just beginning to be considered clichés, but they remain good examples of the kind of language which can be used to smooth the way between items.

There also comes a moment in an event which has been reported for several successive days when it is desirable to resort to easily understood shorthand by way of an opening phrase. In that way, the long drawn out, vastly complicated series of court cases involving the former architect John Poulson became, after a while, merely

The Poulson Affair

and the break-in at the Democratic Party's Washington headquarters, which eventually led to a President's overthrow, was identified as

The Watergate Scandal

long before the revelations ceased. In each case three little words were sufficient to make any viewer sharpen the senses ready for the next instalment of the saga.

In the context of short news programmes, this shorthand is a most effective technique. But there are clear dangers. First there is the assumption it makes of the audience's knowledge of events; second is the case of complicated issues in which the background is all too easily obscured. After a while, for example, the dispute about bonus payments and overtime rates for one hundred of the two thousand workers at the Rusting Cars Company is handily telescoped into

The Rusting Cars strike

A week later, with the dispute escalating into component shortages and lay-offs at other motor factories, the viewer may be forgiven for losing sight of the original problem. So in these cases it is necessary to go back over the entire ground, however much some editors might consider it a waste of precious air-time.

But, whether it concerns an old event or new, the writer's aim must always be to ensure that an opening sentence of any vision story hits the target first time. The viewer must be properly alerted to matters of interest and importance by the skilled use of words which, in effect, have the newsreader bawling: "Hey, you! Watch *this*!"

Illustration—the use of stills

The first stage in making the simple vision story more interesting (and the point at which television begins to exploit its inherent advantage) comes with the addition of *stills*. These take the place of the newsreader's image on the screen, while the voice continues to add information.

Some television organisations use the word *caption* as a generic term for all non-moving illustration. In BBC Television News the still is *photographic* material: a 35 mm colour slide, a colour or black and white print, or a self-developing picture taken by an instant-picture camera.

At one time, the stock 'personality' pictures to be found in television news departments resembled the dull, full-face 'mug-shots' usually seen in police records or the pages of passports (Fig. 1). Fortunately, mainly as a result of the spread of colour television in the late sixties and early seventies, there has been an opportunity for a complete re-think. As a result, those ugly passport snaps have largely given way to bright, natural, frequently unposed, pictures taken by photographers mindful of the television screen format, which is wider than it is high (Fig. 2).

The bulk of these are 35 mm colour transparencies, although a percentage of colour prints, including instant pictures for speed, are also used, and such bodies as government departments, embassies, specialist and trade libraries provide a mixture of shapes, sizes and qualities, often without charge.

The international picture agencies, while remaining easily the most important source of black and white prints, particularly from abroad, are now also able to transmit *colour* pictures by wire through a tri-colour separation process. An original colour picture is re-photographed successively through red, green and blue filters, and the results sent over the wire. In the darkroom at the receiving end the original scene is reconstituted in full colour by applying the same process in reverse.

Rather less complicated and cheaper methods of building libraries of stills include the re-photographing and enlargement of individual frames of 16mm cine colour film to produce a print size and quality adequate for television news transmission purposes. An alternative use of 16mm film is to stop it at a pre-selected point on its way through telecine, and to give what is known as a *still frame*. But this has the disadvantage of engaging (for only marginal benefit) machinery which may be in short supply and needed for other purposes.[1]

With proper care on the part of the cameraman, still photographic prints can be filmed quite successfully using an ordinary 16mm camera in the conventional way: really detailed close-ups call for the use of a *rostrum unit*, in essence a movable film camera mounted above a flat surface. Pans, zooms, tilts and other camera movements and exposures can be controlled with extreme precision to provide pleasing results over areas even as small as those offered by the 35mm format. But, as the film has then to be processed and edited in the normal way, the operation is slow.

News stills are usually transmitted directly by placing them on stands or by pinning them up in the studio on boards within sight of the electronic cameras, or by feeding them into modified projector-cameras known as *scanners*. Small areas can also be shown with the use of a *micro-scanner*, a mounted camera capable of being moved up and down on the same principle as the photographic enlarger.

Making the choice

In many respects it is far easier to choose a still from a strictly limited range, for if there exists in a department only one portrait

---

[1]Not all telecine machines are capable of reproducing still frames.

picture of a particular subject the decision is confined to a straight choice between using it or not.

Headaches begin with the vast libraries. These are 150,000 35 mm colour slides alone in the BBC Central Stills Department in west London. Such luxury demands the newswriter's intimate knowledge of each subject as it arises, for no one else is in a position to decide which of the available stills most aptly match the mood. Such judgements may be as basic as ensuring that a report about increased taxation is *not* illustrated by a smiling portrait of the finance minister who has just announced them. That decisions even as simple as this are needed only goes to show what traps exist for the unwary.

For while there can be (and have been) legal implications in straightforward mistakes of identification, even where the matter of identity is not disputed, a writer's preference for one particular still over another could lead to charges of distortion. Take the astonishing change of physical appearance from the confident, PR-man's Richard Nixon fresh from re-election, to the hollow-cheeked president facing the immediate consequences of Watergate.

For instance, in reporting matters connected with his memoirs, who could say with certainty which stock picture most accurately represents the *real* Nixon? It may not be a case of simply choosing the most recent photograph, although constant attention must also be paid to such apparently trivial detail as general appearance and changes in clothing and hair-style.

George Best, at the height of his soccer-playing fame, seemed to be alternately bearded and clean-shaven week by week. Even if the journalists had difficulty in keeping up to date, the aficionados of the game had no doubts, and were quick to pounce on British television news services foolhardy enough to choose the wrong style for the wrong week.

Writing to stills

A news photograph should appear on the screen for no fewer than five seconds (15 words). Three seconds are about the absolute minimum, otherwise the image appears to flash in front of the viewer's eyes and disappear again before the information can be assimilated. The *maximum* time depends very much on the subject.

A fairly 'busy' action shot of casualties being carried by stretcher away from a car crash needs longer to register than a library portrait of a well-known politician, but it is fairly safe to assume that a ten second shot is long enough in most cases. Economics add an exception to the rule: a photograph bought for a large sum because of its exclusiveness or rarity value should be exploited fully even though the picture itself (say, the last one taken of someone now missing) might be unremarkable. To dismiss this valuable property in a brief five or six seconds of air-time would be wasteful.

However long it is held on the screen, every still should be used to its maximum advantage, by introducing it into the narrative at a point which helps to add definite emphasis to the story. It must not be allowed to drift in, apparently at random, causing moments of confusion for the viewer:

> Referring to the . . .
>
> (up still of Prime Minister)
>
> . . . latest trade deal, the Prime Minister said . . .

Bringing in the picture a few words later makes all the difference:

> Referring to the latest trade deal . . .
>
> (up still of Prime Minister)
>
> . . . the Prime Minister said . . .

The same principle applies to choosing the right moment at which to return to the reader in vision. It is not acceptable to whisk the still from under the viewer's nose without good reason. Much better to wait until the end of a sentence.

Where events call for a sequence of pictures, it is important to maintain a rhythm by keeping each on the screen for approximately the same duration. Six, five and seven seconds would probably be reasonable for three successive stills relating to the same subject; five, twelve and eight would not. The temptation to go back to the reader on camera for a few seconds, between stills, should be avoided, otherwise continuity is broken. In this context, a brief shot of the newsreader becomes *another*, *but unrelated* picture, interrupting the flow. If returning to the newsreader during the sequence becomes unavoidable, it is far better to make the link a deliberately long one.

Writing to a series of stills can, and should be extremely satisfying, particularly when action shots are involved. Unlike newsfilm, where the writer is sometimes a slave to film editing grammar, pictures can be arranged in any required order to suit the script, and even a fairly routine item is capable of being made to look and sound interesting:

> Four men have been rescued from a small boat off the Kent coast. They'd been adrift for twenty four hours after the boat's engine failed during a gale. Their distress call was answered by...

> (bring up Still One, helicopter landing)

> ... a Royal Air Force helicopter, which flew them forty miles to Dover for medical treatment.

> (change to Still Two, man on stretcher).

> The owner of the boat is now in hospital suffering from exposure; the three others have been allowed home.

Apart from the opening news point, the story is told and the pictures shown in chronological order for ease of explanation. Note, too, that the basic rule of television scriptwriting is observed —the commentary *complements* what the pictures show and does not merely repeat what the viwer can see for himself. Still One says where the rescued men were taken and for what purpose; Still Two, while identifying the stretcher case and his condition, does not leave the viewer to wonder about the fate of the others.

From a production point of view it makes sense to go from one still to another in the same sequence by using the same technique, cutting or mixing. The use of an electronic wipe from one to another should be reserved for changes of subject. If programmes are being transmitted in colour it is easier on the eye to use either all colour or all monochrome pictures in one sequence. If they *have* to be mixed, the two types should be shown as separate blocks.

Composites

Composite stills (*split screens*) are effective if used sparingly. In their most common form these consist of two heads, each occupying one half of the screen (Fig. 3). The effect is achieved by physically mounting separate pictures on to one piece of card, or by copying them photographically. For preference, the faces should look slightly inwards towards each other and *not* out of the screen (Fig. 4) and they should be matched in size, style and picture quality, even if it means copying one or both originals.

46

STILLS AND COMPOSITES

Fig. 1. Old style 'mug shot' still.

Fig. 2. New style photograph. Natural and unposed.

Fig. 3. Split screen. Two pictures in one, which must be of similar size and quality. Subjects should look in towards each other. Identify characters left to right.

Fig. 4. Split screen. Uneven composition is bound to create a distraction on the screen.

Fig. 5. Three-way split. Names printed on to avoid confusion.

We must strive to achieve a better balance in the world

Fig. 6. Split-screen quotes. For long quotations a moving roller caption can be used.

Fig. 7. Split screen using still and map.

The commentary identifies the characters from left to right.

A three-way split can be achieved and is sometimes necessary as with trios of astronauts, but here it is perhaps worthwhile to print the individual names on the bottom of the picture to avoid any risk of confusing the viewer (Fig. 5).

Other versions of the split screen have one half of the picture occupied by a photograph, the other by some form of artwork. Written quotations (Fig. 6) and maps (Fig. 7) are particularly popular, and can have considerable impact. A further variation is the *roller caption*. This retains the photographic half of the still while an extended quotation is printed on to the surface of a drum device, its movement controlled to reveal the wording in step with the newsreader's speaking pace.

The capacity to employ such a wide range of styles is an undeniable advantage to television news as part of its job to make programmes interesting as well as informative. Yet, simply because stills are available in such quantities, the danger of 'overkill' is ever-present, and writers must avoid a tendency to use them *automatically*, almost as a reflex action. The fact is that some stories are better told with no illustration other than the newsreader's face.

David Frost had a cruel but accurate comment about the obsession of some television people to try to illustrate everything, however unsuitable. It has become known as the Lord

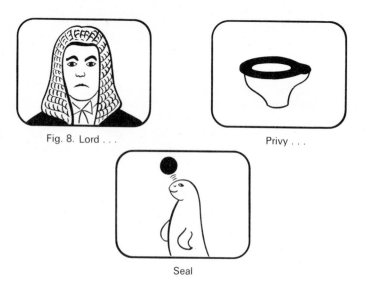

Fig. 8. Lord . . .

Privy . . .

Seal

Privy Seal syndrome, and stands as the perfect, awful warning to anyone lured into the use of pictures just for their own sake.

Adding artwork

Complementing the still photograph is the *caption*, the family name for television news artwork. Its use has clear advantages for journalists passing on information about events in a complicated modern world. Maps help the immediate identification of geographical locations, diagrams and charts further explain details not otherwise easily understood when given by the newsreader alone: series of budget proposals . . . the main conclusions of official reports . . . detailed timetables of events . . . the ups and downs of bank rates and trade figures.

How this artwork is prepared depends on available resources and the extent to which specialist staff and materials can be properly employed. Some local or very small national news services are able to get by perfectly well with part-time artists, either staff members spared briefly from other duties, or design students happy to earn small sums for an hour or two of extra labour of love. In each case the 'studio' usually consists of some handy corner not far from where the newsroom journalists are at work, plus a stock of basic materials such as blank black cards measuring 12 by 9 in (30·48 × 22·86 cm), an atlas, a number of previously used maps and charts outlined in white, pens, pencils, rulers, white paint, brushes, razor blades, scissors and sheets of rub-on, instant lettering in a limited range of type faces and sizes.

Those news departments which have to take their artwork more seriously employ full-time, trained artists working in proper graphics departments furnished with enough sophisticated equipment to provide a service offering both speed and variety. BBC TV News artists have a hot press machine capable of turning out clean, unfussy type in sizes ranging from 36 to 60 pt. Over the years, hundreds of stock maps, all carefully catalogued, have been painted on to card, the place names printed on to removable, transparent plastic cells so that the original outlines beneath remain untouched for re-use. Sketched figures and symbols are also stockpiled as backgrounds for the charts and diagrams in most frequent demand.

In general, the newswriter need not expect to be too much concerned with the fundamentals governing the design of news graphics material, as that would mean encroaching on the artist's own territory. Nevertheless, artwork which may have a screen life of no more than a few seconds must be clear and easy to follow, with bold strokes on unambiguous backgrounds. Some designs, however, which look superb in colour are meaningless to those viewing in black and white.

Knowledge of the dimensional limitations also helps. Among the most important of these is to remember how much information can be squeezed on to a standard 12×9 in caption, bearing in mind that unnecessary clutter reduces visual impact, and that a small area all round the edge is automatically lost in the process of transmission. This *cut-off*, which effectively reduces the caption surface, applies to every television set, and is exaggerated on receivers which have poorly adjusted pictures. All this adds to the journalist's problem in deciding the wording to go on charts, and particularly affects the name and title superimpositions which occupy the bottom third of the screen, these the most common forms of artwork used in television news.

Not only is it a matter of sometimes trying to squash too much into a limited width, so that cut-off inevitably mutilates each end of the lettering, the information occupies so much room that part of the accompanying illustration itself is also obscured (Fig. 9).

Fig. 9.

Smaller lettering would be difficult to read, so the alternative solution (Fig. 10) is much better, as it occupies only two lines, one of which is an abbreviation of the title.

Above all, the newswriter using the Graphic Artist's skill to

50

Fig. 10.

illustrate a story must anticipate how the accompanying commentary will be structured. There is little point in commissioning good-looking charts full of important details to which no reference is made, or in cramming beautifully-scaled maps with place names which the script ignores to the consternation of the viewer, who is then left wondering why they were put there in the first place.

The temptation to add anything except the strictly relevant must be resisted. Take the report of our bank raid (page 40). A map illustrating the location of Luton needs only the additional reference points of London and the most important trunk road, the M1, to give a clear idea of the town's position in southern England (Fig. 11). The arbitrary addition of several other big cities and county names may make the map look more attractive to some eyes, but it would produce total confusion in the viewer during its few seconds on the screen (Fig. 12).

At the other extreme, a large-scale map showing Luton completely isolated from everywhere else in the country is just as valueless (Fig. 13).

The key to success in writing to graphics lies in the assembly of words in sequences which lead the viewer's eye progressively across the material from left to right, top to bottom. But it is not enough to repeat orally what appears on the screen. Some supplementary information must be fed in as well, but if, through carelessness, too wide a difference is allowed to develop between what the viewer is being told and being shown, the effect that writer and artist have been at pains to create will be destroyed.

51

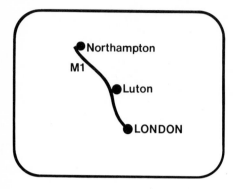

Fig. 11. Enough detail to give the viewer a point of reference during the few seconds the map is on the screen.

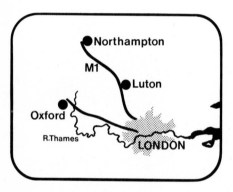

Fig. 12. A prettier map, but the extra place names are of no help unless some reference is made to them.

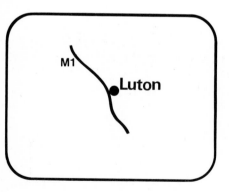

Fig. 13. The other extreme. No reference point to give any idea how Luton relates to the rest of the country.

Fig. 14. Simple charts help to get figures across. Accompanying commentary must lead the viewer's eye from left to right, top to bottom (see also Fig. 16).

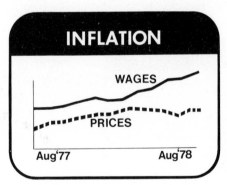

Fig. 15. Diagrams and graphs follow same pattern of simplicity. Extra information can be given in the script.

That is inevitable with even the most simple illustrations:

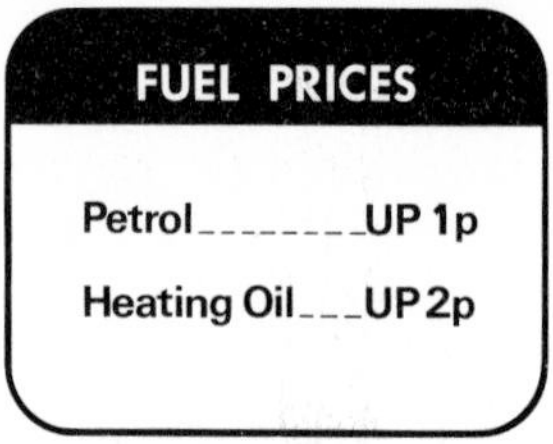

FUEL PRICES

Petrol _____ UP 1p

Heating Oil ___ UP 2p

Fig. 16. (a)

"Two pence goes on oil for central heating, making it 40 pence a gallon. One penny is put on petrol to make it 95 pence a gallon."

By transposing the two sentences of commentary, some improvement is achieved, but not a complete cure:

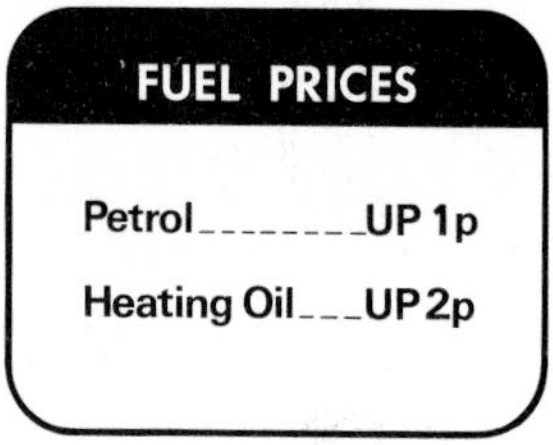

FUEL PRICES

Petrol _____ UP 1p

Heating Oil ___ UP 2p

Fig. 16. (b)

"One penny is put on petrol to make it 95 pence a gallon. Two pence goes on oil for central heating, making it 40 pence a gallon."

Far better to use the same phraseology as on the chart, and in the same order, so that there is no conflict between words and picture:

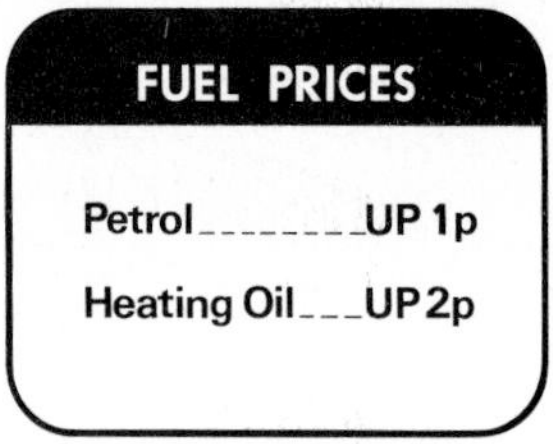

FUEL PRICES

Petrol _____ UP 1p

Heating Oil ___ UP 2p

Fig. 16. (c)

"Petrol goes up by one penny a gallon to 95 pence. Central heating oil goes up by two pence a gallon to 40 pence."

Probably the most obviously devoted adherents to this discipline are the makers of television commercials, who have very similar periods of screen time in which to establish unambiguous links between the visual and the oral. The technique is particularly necessary on occasions where information is added to a piece of artwork, one stage at a time, by the use of superimpositions and animations.[1] So, in the example, the first spoken

---

[1] Superimpositions are achieved by mixing two sources *electronically* to produce one picture. Animations are *mechanical*. The extra information is hidden under tabs or flaps which are slid back at the appropriate moment during transmission.

sentence would accompany one fact on the chart:

FUEL PRICES

Petrol _____ UP 1p

"Petrol goes up by one penny a gallon to 95 pence."

The next would be said simultaneously with the introduction of the second stage, to complete the picture:

FUEL PRICES

Petrol _____ UP 1p

Heating Oil ___ UP 2p

"Central heating oil goes up by two pence a gallon to 40 pence."

The newswriter's responsibilities do not end with the written commentary. Completed artwork must be carefully checked against any original plans, however sketchy, and where sequences of captions are involved, no doubts left about the exact order of transmission. To have one illustration on the screen while the commentary is clearly referring to another is hardly likely to inspire the audience's confidence; mis-spellings, which somehow seem to occur in only the most simple, everyday words, have a tendency to harvest bulging post-bags of complaint.

It is true that genuine variations do exist in the spelling of certain place names, particularly where they are transliterations. Most recently, the Middle East and south-east Asia have provided problems, as spellings in news agency reports have often differed widely from those in atlases or gazetteers. To the domestic audience, it may scarcely matter which is used as long as there is consistency. The solution to all these problems is to adopt certain standard reference books (*The Times Atlas*, the *Oxford Dictionary*, etc.) as the arbiters and ignore everything else.

For plain reasons of speed and simplicity, most television news artwork styles are very basic, and likely to remain so, although even here, despite frequent pressures of time, innovations have emerged, particularly in 'one-off' street plans and animated drawings. Advances have been made, too, in the use of models, partly as a direct outcome of the need to interpret incidents of war or urban terrorism. Some computerised lettering systems are in use, and although these have advantages, particularly in the matter of speed, the results I have seen so far are much less attractive for straight news work than those produced manually. More importantly, such expensive installations are likely to be considered justifiable only by those few organisations unable to resist change.

What may alter somewhat earlier is the convention that all artwork (and stills too) must conform to the four by three ratio. At present some news organisations simply refuse to use pictures which are in the wrong format to fill the screen.

But an interesting theory is put forward by Bertil Allander of the Swedish Broadcasting Corporation. Discussing the whole question of perspective, he suggests[1] that there is positive value in breaking with standard methods.

The television screen, he believes, is capable of accepting all kinds of formats, and there must be times "when one will cheerfully accept a smaller picture in order to get a neater composition or add to the expressiveness of the format". At all events, says Allander, "it must surely be unnecessary to fill up a picture with uninteresting material for the sake of the format and, into the bargain, run the risk of leading the viewer's eye astray".

Certainly, the application of that principle would immediately make way for a whole new range of shapes at present considered unacceptable.

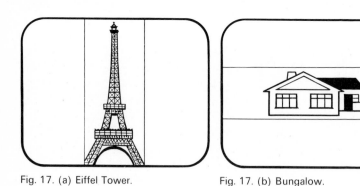

Fig. 17. (a) Eiffel Tower.   Fig. 17. (b) Bungalow.

---

[1] "... *it's not reality any more*". (Swedish Broadcasting Corporation, 1974).

Finally, on the subject of stills and graphics, it is worthwhile remembering that any illustration of this type is also an extremely useful means of visual punctuation within a programme. Ending an item with a still picture, map or chart, presents the ideal opportunity to return to the newsreader for an entirely fresh subject.

Pictures and tape sound

So far the emphasis has been on the introduction of visual material to accompany words spoken by the newsreader in the studio. Now comes the moment to create a temporary but complete replacement for the reader by the use of sound-only reports.

These are the blood brothers of the dispatches which have become the stock-in-trade of radio news programmes all over the world. For television, telephoned or radioed sound reports, whether 'live' or recorded on to magnetic tape, come a poor second to newsfilm or other forms of illustration. But the nature of world news demands that the voice of the reporter on the spot is, on many occasions, infinitely preferable to the alternative of nothing at all.

That said, the newswriter's main considerations in dealing with such material revolve around three main factors: quality, duration and illustration.

Where sound *quality* is concerned, high standards of intelligibility are required, and technical staff are usually at hand to say at once whether atmospherics or other forms of interference make a report technically usable. But there are times when sound of *any* sort merits inclusion. Those early reports from space, for example, were scarcely intelligible, but this did not detract in the least from their news value. Even now, where reports are themselves of intrinsic worth, despite lack of clarity, the answer is not to discard them but to assist the viewer by 'translating' the spoken words into captions for displaying simultaneously on the screen.

Bigger problems arise on those borderline occasions when the voice quality is rather open to question. Here, the trap into which it is too easy to fall is for the newswriter to listen to a recorded dispatch several times (usually through highly-sophisticated equipment) and *then* be convinced that audiences will be able to understand words they will hear only once. In these cases, the long-established journalistic test of 'when in doubt, leave out',

PICTURES WITH TAPE SOUND

Fig. 18. Composite still to cover voice-only report usually consists of identification of correspondent and location. Difficulty arises when a dispatch is made from one place about events taking place in another.

should be even more rigorously applied, and the dispatch used as a source of information for quotation by the newsreader.

The question of *duration* must be left open for individuals to decide for themselves in the light of each report's significance. But, in drawing up broad guidelines, remember that sound reports are invariably lengthy, as they are primarily intended for radio news outlets, with any use by television purely incidental. It is desirable to go only so far in adopting intact, techniques of one medium for use in another.

One way out is to encourage reporters to send extra, shorter pieces especially for use in television programmes constructing them so that they cover any visual material which may become available at a later stage. Where this is not possible, intelligent editing can make a dispatch more suitable. Straightforward factual material is omitted and then condensed for the news-reader's introduction: what remain are the descriptive passages conveying atmosphere.

This leads to the final difficulty in finding relevant *illustration* to accompany the sound. As it is considered unacceptable to put either a blank screen or the newsreader's face in front of the viewer while the report is being heard, an attempt must be made to offer something else visually relevant. Fashions change, but current thinking envisages a specially-made composite caption identifying the location from which the report is being made, and the person who is making it (Fig. 18).

This apparently ideal solution poses its own problems, particularly when, as often happens, reporters are calling from one place with information they have gathered about events taking place in another.

How individual newswriters deal with that circumstance depends on a straight choice between what is accurate . . . and what is clear.

WORDS AND MOVING PICTURES

Introduction to film

THE power to transmit moving pictures, whether colour or black and white, 'live' or recorded, through film or electronic means, sets television apart from all its rivals in the business of disseminating news about world events.

For the newcomer embarking on the acquisition of the basic skills to cope with this extra dimension, two major hurdles bar the way. First, and most important, is the need to develop an instinct for the construction of written commentaries in a way which allows the viewer to draw full value from both words and pictures. Second comes the requirement for at least a rudimentary knowledge of how film and videotape work. Each has its own mystique, particularly film, about which enough has been written to sink a whole fleet of proverbial battleships. In every library, shelves groan under a weight of material (much of it by masters of feature and documentary work) sufficient to occupy the keen student for years.

It is not necessary for every newswriter to go that far. But it clearly *is* important to know that, with ingenuity and imagination, film and videotape are tools which are capable of being wielded with real delicacy, even within the larger blunt instrument which is the routine television news programme. Many television journalists, equipped with a high level of these skills, have gone on to find success in other areas of television demanding the subtle use of pictures on one hand with qualities of journalistic hard-headedness on the other.

To begin with, it helps to appreciate the nature of the medium if it is understood that the term 'moving film' is really a misnomer. What the cine camera does is to take a rapid series of *still* pictures which, if run through a projector at the same speed, deceives the human eye into believing that the movement is continuous. In the case of British television, these individual still pictures (called 'frames') are taken and projected at a rate of twenty five per second; in the United States, twenty four.

As for the hardware, television newsfilm makers began to turn to 16 mm cameras and equipment for everyday use in the 1950's. Although 16 mm has long since been universal in news for TV, until that time experts were convinced that results from anything smaller than the 35 mm format used for cinema feature films were not of sufficient quality for professional showing. Peter Beggin, one of the BBC's veteran, award-winning news cameramen, recalls that the makers of the first 16 mm camera he was issued with were so sure of its use by non-professionals that the instruction booklet included something along the following lines: 'Having placed the camera on the tripod, seat your daughter at the piano, making sure that you are at least five feet away from the subject, and that sufficient light is available from the window'.

Even if that is an apocryphal story, it does accurately reflect the way in which 16 mm was then regarded. Since those days, the format has become widely accepted for television news and documentary work worldwide. It is relatively portable and easy to handle compared with the cumbersome 35 mm cameras of cinema newsreel days and, probably more than anything else, has been responsible for making the viewer feel personally involved in the action taking place on the screen.

Some television services have been experimenting with an even smaller gauge, Super 8, in common use for home movies, but for all its lightness and economy there is no sign that the world's major television news organisations are about to make the switch from the bigger brother. Any change is likely to be out of film altogether and into electronic news gathering, as the major American networks have already begun to demonstrate.

While the tendency has been for television to go for smaller gauges, the feature film industry has largely maintained its devotion to 35 mm or even large formats. But with certain types of programme, some similarity with technical practice in the commercial cinema does remain. This is in the type of film exposed in the camera. It is a *negative*, from which positive prints are 'struck' after chemical processing. While the original negative is then stored safely under laboratory conditions to prevent any accidental mishandling, work goes ahead on viewing the 'rushes', preliminary unedited sections of material chosen by the director from any number of re-takes of the same scene.

The rushes are taken away and assembled by a film editor into approximately the shape and length required by the director. This version is called the *rough cut*, which may then be altered or shortened still further until the director is completely satisfied. At this point the original negative is produced from the laboratory and cut precisely to match the cutting copy. From that negative which, in the case of a feature film might represent an investment of millions of pounds in writing, directing and acting talent, any number of prints may be made for showing, all 'graded' in the laboratory to even out any slight variations in the cameraman's original exposure.

The result is that films made by this method are without extreme fluctuations of light and shade from one scene to another, and so are easy on the eye. The negatives, free of dust, breaks or scratches, are always available for further prints to be made without loss of quality. The major drawback is that this system is comparatively slow, and in news time is a luxury which can rarely be afforded.

It was for this single reason that television news and some other topical television programmes decided long ago to cut out as many of the intermediate stages as possible between the exposure of the film material and its transmission. This was achieved by the simple expedient of taking the developed *original* material straight from the camera and transmitting that. In adopting this method, television news people had to accept the very real risk that a careless or unlucky film editor, working quickly with much-used equipment, might do irreparable harm to precious material, and that in some circumstances an edit once made might be impossible to restore. That in turn put greater responsibility on the *editorial* staff to ensure that the right decisions about editing the film were made first time.

To add to the difficulties, film editors and newswriters working for stations transmitting only black and white pictures had to make their decisions based on identification of people and events from film viewed in *negative*, as delivered by the processing department. After a while, experience taught that it was possible to recognise the better known public figures. But all too often a certain amount of guesswork was involved. Fortunately, the viewer was spared such mysteries. During the film's transmission stage all was put right by the use of what was called 'phase reversal,' an electronic means of changing the blacks to white and the whites to black, thus producing a normal positive image.

This particular problem did not accompany the switch from monochrome to colour filming, which began in the sixties. After much discussion and experiment, many news services opted for film type Ektachrome EF 7242, made by Kodak. The chief characteristic of this film was that it was a 'reversal' stock, which meant that once it had been through the processing plant it appeared in the same form as the amateur photographer's 35 mm colour transparency, as a *positive* for projection without further chemical development.

Since then, rivals to EF 7242 have appeared on the scene in the shape of RT 100 and RT 400, faster reversal stocks made in Japan by Fuji and a series of three from Agfa-Gevaert of West Germany. The 7242 stock itself is being phased out by Kodak in favour of their own EF 7240 or VNF (Video News Film). All these types, now in wide use, can also be 'force processed' to make feasible an effective increase of up to three stops in film speed. This latitude allows the cameraman to continue filming even when lighting conditions are quite poor.

After processing in the laboratory, reversal originals can be taken directly to the cutting room for editing. As with mono-chrome negative there exists the danger that an editor working hurriedly with late material will accidentally damage the film surface, although chemical pre-hardening reduces the risk. Where superficial scratches *are* inflicted repair is sometimes possible by a wax coating process, but this takes longer than the breed of anxious television newspeople are usually prepared to wait.

Film sound

Although for some years it has been both technically feasible and considered ethical to add studio sound effects to silent news film, by far the happier solution is to record the sound at the same time as the picture, on location. This is the system widely adopted by the major television news services despite the cost of main-taining a second member of the film unit, a sound recordist, and the necessary equipment.

The sound equipment itself, usually purchased separately, has to be chosen to match one of two camera systems. The first, invariably used in feature and non-news television filming, is known as *double system* (otherwise *separate magnetic—Sepmag*) or *synchronous sound* (sync sound). Here the cameraman takes the pictures while the recordist captures the sound on a sophisti-cated tape recorder consuming $\frac{1}{4}$ in magnetic tape of the sort used on the reel-to-reel recorders on sale all over the world. To ensure that, on transmission, lip movements fit precisely with the spoken words, sounds and pictures have to be recorded at a constant speed, and this is achieved by an electronic device locking camera and recorder motor together when they are operated.

The double system has a number of advantages, among them the high quality of the recording, and the fact that the sound is capable of being checked immediately by replaying the tape as on a conventional recorder. The disadvantage is that as a result of the need to ensure sound and picture synchronisation every time the camera is switched on, it can be a relatively slow operation in the field. Back in the office the film is developed separately, while the $\frac{1}{4}$ in tape has to be re-recorded on to 16 mm film coated with ferrous oxide.

Probably the more popular system for television news sound filming continues to be the *single system* (*combined magnetic* or *Commag*). Here the sound is recorded on to a narrow stripe of the oxide material which is bonded to one edge of the raw film during manufacture.

In the field, a portable amplifier does away with the need for a separate tape recorder. But there are two shortcomings. First, the sound quality is not as good as in the double system, and second, problems are presented at the editing stage. This is because the sound recording mechanism inside the camera is fitted a distance equivalent on 16 mm, to 28 frames away from the picture gate. This enables the rapid stop-start movement of the film to be evened out during exposure.

Where editing is not required, no problems arise, as the telecine machine used to transmit the film has a similar 28-frame gap between sound reproduction and picture heads. Where editing is necessary, however, the film editor must make his cut remembering that the sound is *ahead* of the accompanying picture by just over one second. However skilfully it is done, a commag cut is generally ugly, and far more satisfactory results are achieved by re-recording the sound on to the same 16 mm track as used in the double system. Cuts can then be made much more easily, although it means of course that picture and sound have to be edited separately, and that extra care must be taken to avoid loss of synchronism between the two elements.

In the cutting room

In an ideal situation, the television newswriter would be able to sit at ease and watch the developed 'rushes' of the film on a

64

16mm FILM TYPES

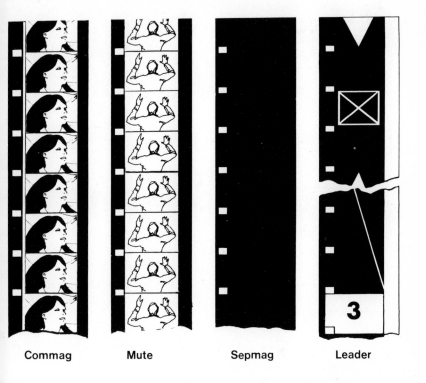

Commag **Mute** **Sepmag** **Leader**

Fig. 19. Commag—film is edged with magnetic stripe for sound, which is 28 frames (just over one sec.) ahead of picture.
Mute—used in double system of recording.
Sepmag track—exactly the same width as film. Sound can be re-recorded from commag stripe (single system) or quarter inch tape (double system).
Film leader—usually calibrated in seconds, to ensure exact synchronisation of sound and picture. Moving numbers help coutdown on transmission.

FILM SOUND SYSTEMS COMPARED

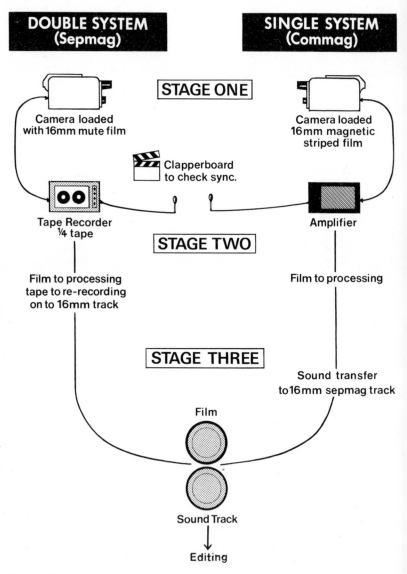

The double system, although slow in operation, ensures the best quality results. The single system, recorded on the actual camera material is still the more popular method for television news work.

screen big enough to appreciate all that the cameraman has accomplished. Unfortunately, on most occasions, newswriter and film editor go directly into a cutting room with their reels of film and sound track, and find themselves working against the clock, able only to make instinctive decisions about material they may have time to see just once—and that at double normal speed.

What they select depends on the nature of the subject, its interest, importance, and nominated duration within the programme. Equally important on occasion is the extent to which the two have briefed themselves, so that by the time the film is cleared from processing they are already aware of the contents and have planned a rough scheme for editing.

At this stage there is no room for clashes of interest or temperament. Instead, only teamwork to ensure that what appears on the screen, perhaps just a few minutes later, reflects the successful fusion of separate professional skills.

In recent years this has become more possible than ever before, as relationships between film editors and writers are less strained than they once were. Most of the old-style cutters who originally left the film industry to join the pioneers of television news have now departed. With them has gone much of the friction which arose with writers who felt that getting the story across was always more important than sticking to some of the more rigid rules of film editing grammar.

The old school has been replaced by a new breed of young film editors who acknowledge that they and the newswriters share one common aim—to tell the story, in pictures and words, as coherently as possible. The result is modern, streamlined and effective. Not that the younger film editors are any more keen than their predecessors to break the rules. It is just that for the sake of simplicity they are prepared to dispense with the irrelevant.

This has tended to increase the flow of expertise in unexpected directions, and those writers with a developed sense of things visual need no longer be surprised or upset when an enthusiastic film editor with a feeling for words suggests a possible line for the commentary. So, in many ways, it has blossomed into a genuine, two-way relationship, in which more is expected of the film editor than the slavish cutting of film to editorial orders. And it remains significant that in the best-ordered news services the commentary is planned around the pictures, and not vice-versa.

In general, as may already be apparent, the film editor's greatest problem in television news is very much the same as that of his editorial counterpart—lack of space in which to tell the story. Yet it is really remarkable how much can be told in 30 sec of screen time. This represents probably no more than six or seven separate shots cut together in a skilful way to ensure that the film will appear just as complete and coherent if dug out of the archives next year as when viewed on the air in an hour's time.

Sometimes the choice of material may be so limited as to make the film editor's task a matter of simple assembly. Much depends on the cameraman who, given a reasonable amount of time on location, aims to provide a variety of shots for selection. The editing itself takes place in a specially equipped, darkened room, of which there may be several, according to the needs of the organisation (Fig. 20). The most important and expensive piece of machinery is the editing machine, frequently one of two makes, *Acmade* (United Kingdom) or *Steenbeck* (West Germany). Each is a highly sophisticated system, capable of showing the film on a small, integral screen, and reproducing the sound, whether of the combined magnetic or separate magnetic variety, through a compact amplifier (Fig. 21).

Further refinements enable picture or sound to be speeded up, slowed down, run backwards or forwards, or stopped and started at any point to allow editing precisely to the frame. There are counters for measuring the film in either feet, or minutes and seconds.

As the newswriter watches, the editor goes through all the sound and picture material, checking for content and quality. Together they discuss the general outline, building up a mental picture of the sequence of events. Applying a grease pencil to the film surface, the editor marks the beginning and ending of each chosen shot. Later, when all the film has been viewed, the pencil marks become the guide by which the editor breaks out the individual shots by hand, hanging them up into roughly the order into which they will be joined, on to pins fixed in a wooden frame (Fig. 22). This, in turn, is attached to a bin lined with cloth to avoid damaging the surface of the film.

The next most important piece of equipment in the cutting room is the device for joining the selected shots in the correct order. Two types are in common use. One is the *cement joiner* (Fig. 23a), often a bulky table top model incorporating a heavy metal clamp operated by foot pedal. The two ends of the film are prepared for joining by scraping away some of the surface and applying the special liquid cement with a small brush. The clamp

FILM EDITING

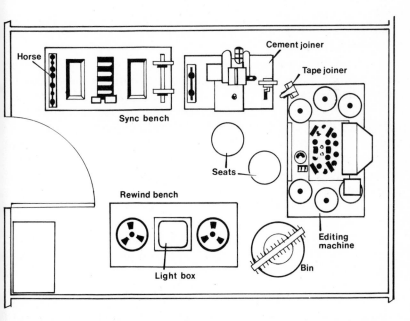

Fig. 20. Film editor at work on a editing machine, and layout of a typical cutting room.

is then used to keep pressure on the overlapping join for about ten seconds until the cement hardens.

The alternative editing device is altogether smaller, in principle resembling the splicer used for sound tape editing (Fig. 23b). Here the ends are cut square, butted together and joined with transparent adhesive tape. Each method has its devotees. While the overlap-cement join is said to be stronger, it is certainly slower to make. The tape join can be unpicked easily enough without damaging the film, so alterations are less difficult to make. But tape joins are inclined to stretch if the film is projected too often, and tell-tale jumps appear between edits.

Long and complicated film stories, especially those where sound or the overlay technique is involved (see page 131), may take several hours to put together, and the newswriter will probably leave the film editor to return to the newsroom and other chores. At some stage the writer may be called back to give an opinion as editing progresses but, as often as not, there is no further contact between the two until the film editor's work is completed. Then, after running the film through, a decision is taken at once about whether the cut version comes up to expectations or whether changes or trims are necessary.

Shot-listing

Once satisfied, the newswriter's next step represents what is undoubtedly the most critical point in the entire operation to ensure that, on transmission, the written commentary matches the edited pictures.

This is called *shot-listing*, which consists of noting details of the length, picture and sound content of every individual scene in the edited film, at this stage usually referred to as a *cut story*. What makes the process even more important is, as we shall see at a later stage, that news programmes are among the very few still transmitted 'live' and that there is usually only one chance for the newswriter to find out whether his script is accurate, and that is on transmission.

Shot-listing procedure is simplicity itself, however long the film, although for this example, we will take a typical, but imaginary 30 sec. story about the arrival of a party leader for a political conference.

The film editor sets the counter on the machine to zero to coincide with the opening frame of the first shot. At the end of the first join the machine is stopped so that the newswriter can

FILM EDITING EQUIPMENT

Fig. 21. Editing machine.

Fig. 22. Editing bin.

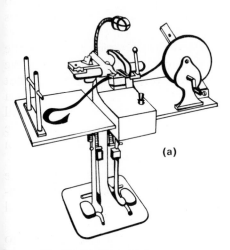

(a)

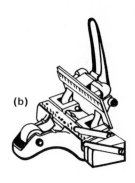

(b)

Fig. 23. (a) Cement joiner.

Fig. 23. (b) Tape joiner.

put down on paper everything the scene contains, together with the clock time at the end of the first shot, say, three seconds:

GV (general view) exterior of conference hall . . . 3 sec.

The editing machine is restarted and the film runs on until the end of the next shot, which lasts four seconds. The newswriter makes a note of the details and the *cumulative time:*

MS (medium shot) delegates arriving on foot . . . 7 sec.

This operation is repeated until the end of the film is reached and the newswriter's shot-list looks like this:

GV Exterior of conference hall	....	3 sec.
MS Delegates arriving on foot	....	7 sec.
CU (close up) Crowds waiting	....	10 sec.
LS (long shot) Leader's car turns corner	....	15 sec.
MS Motorcycle escort dismounts	....	18 sec.
CU Car door opens, leader gets out	....	24 sec.
GV Leader walks up steps into building	....	30 sec.

Armed with those details back in the newsroom, the newswriter will be able to time a reference to the party leader to the precise moment, 18 seconds from the start of the film, when the car door opens and that familiar figure appears. Without that information to hand, accurate scripting would be impossible.

Often, when time is pressing, the temptation is to skimp shot-listing and rely on the memory. It never works. Even if it means nagging the film editor into more viewings, the newswriter must be absolutely certain that before leaving the cutting room for the newsroom the shot-list is complete down to the last detail. Going back to see the film again later before transmission is at best difficult, at worst impossible.

Writing to film

The mechanics of writing any sort of film commentary can be explained and understood in about an hour. To apply them *well* requires a special ability to appreciate exactly the value moving pictures have in relation to the words necessary to complement them.

Writing to *news* film is a distillation of that particular skill which some journalists, despite a genuine feeling for words and sympathy for pictures, never quite develop. Exactly what it is that separates the excellent from the merely acceptable is virtually impossible to distinguish without the impact of the pictures themselves. Looking at the written script by itself will provide no clue. Fowler would have shuddered at the use of two-word, verbless, inverted sentences and the apparently casual regard for punctuation. The test is to ignore the printed page and to sit back, listen and watch as the commentary adds a delicate counterpoint to the pictures on the screen.

Probably the first mistake the novice news scriptwriter makes is to try to cram into 30 sec. of screen time the maximum number of facts that previous journalistic experience has taught as being essential. The result will be total chaos. The script takes little or no notice of the film it was meant to accompany; the style is heavy, as written for the printed page and, most likely, the news-reader will come a poor second in the oral sprint to finish the commentary before the pictures end.

At three words to the second, a 30 sec. film gives the writer a maximum of 90 words to play with. No matter how cleverly they are used, there is no way in which it is possible to squeeze in more and still expect the commentary to make any sense to those hearing it.

From the outset, the newswriter must learn to exercise a ruthless economy of words, first so that the pictures are able to do their work properly and, secondly, to avoid the ultimate sin of having the film run out while the newsreader is still speaking. It is far safer to under-write and leave a few seconds of pictures un-scripted.

Most beginners' commentaries tend to refer in great detail to people, places or events which do not appear on the film. This is, in many ways, an understandable fault, but one which must be corrected at once. Over the years the viewer has come to recognise such references as signposts leading to whatever is coming next on the film, and is bound to feel cheated if, in the end, the signs lead nowhere.

Too much detail has, equally, the effect of drawing attention to what may be missing from film coverage. A blow-by-blow account of cars screaming to a halt, armed men tumbling out and shots being fired during a jewel robbery should be avoided when all the camera is able to record in the aftermath is a solitary policeman walking over broken glass from a window, a few specks of blood on the floor and tyre marks on the road. The atmosphere can be conveyed just as effectively without using words which make the viewer feel let down that the action is not taking place on the screen.

Similarly with sound: 'cheering' crowds, 'screaming' jet engines, the 'crackle' of small arms fire—all conjure up definite mental pictures. If the viewer does not hear what is generally accepted as a cheer, scream or crackle, the suspicion may arise that the television people do not really know what they are about. Exactly the same response will be evoked by talk of the 'booming' of artillery when what can be heard quite clearly on the film sound track is, indeed, the authentic crackle of small arms fire.

In such cases the newswriter is well advised to use general words less liable to misinterpretation. After all, 'gunfire' is a term capable of being applied to virtually anything between a few pistol shots and a full-scale battle.

Having learned these early lessons, the new newswriter's next mistake will be to write a film commentary which reads rather like a series of newspaper captions. With every change of shot, the viewer is treated to nothing more or less than a verbal repetition of the sights and sounds unfolding on the television screen a few feet away. Thus, the newswriter's influence is as good as meaningless, especially where the script includes clumsy phrases to ensure that the viewer does not escape even the obvious:

"As you can see here . . ."

"The Prime Minister, on the right . . ."

True, there are occasions when it is necessary to take the viewer metaphorically by the scruff of the neck:

"The Smiths knew nothing of the explosion until they returned home a week later. Then, all they found . . . was *this*".

But it is a technique to be used sparingly. In most cases, just to recite what is happening on the film is to lose a great opportunity of telling the viewer something worthwhile. Where the newswriter's skill lies is in being able to convey atmosphere *not* obvious from the pictures.

Take almost any international conference. Ten minutes after the routine photocall, during which delegates are seen talking and joking, a furious row breaks out in the privacy of the closed session. Probably all the newswriter will ever have to work with is film material suggesting that all was sweetness and light. Instead of throwing away the apparently irrelevant, the newswriter should be able to make a virtue of the scenes of accord, singling them out to pinpoint the contrast between events occurring before and during the conference:

> "but the spirit of co-operation didn't last long. Almost as soon as the conference got under way . . ."

'Old' newsfilm, arriving perhaps a day or so after the event, poses a similar test of scriptwriting ingenuity. To re-tell known events exactly as they occurred may be valuable on some rare occasions but, more often than not, the newswriter is faced with the daunting prospect of matching the apparently unmatchable— out of date pictures and up to date facts. The temptation here is probably to 'talk against picture', to ignore what the film contains in order to get most of the facts across. This *can* be done for very brief periods in the commentary, but the technique needs careful judgement to ensure that words and pictures do meet often enough to avoid confusion.

The classic example is that of the library clip which is considered the only piece of film material even vaguely appropriate for the occasion, like the shots of the South American president reviewing troops on Independence Day which have to be used one year later to cover the news that he has been overthrown.

Armed with current agency tape, a few background cuttings and a carefully-made shot-list, the newswriter should be able to tell the story simply enough, even though the film and the words accompanying it are nothing special. Imagine that some of the details of the coup have already been given in vision:

Film Details	Cumulative Time	Commentary
Long shot, troops marching through city centre	0 sec.	It's not even a year since army leaders pledged their loyalty to the civilian government.
Medium shot infantry passing	6 sec.	Then they promised to stay out of domestic politics, whatever the result of the elections. But in the capital today
Medium shot tank column	13 sec.	the tanks were out to enforce a curfew and people were ordered to

Film Details	Cumulative Time	Commentary
Long shot crowds waving	17 sec.	listen to the state radio for an official announcement.
General view government ministers on saluting base	20 sec.	Most of the leading politicians are now under house arrest, although what's happened to the
C/U president on platform	25 sec.	president isn't clear. He's reported to have had warning of the coup
GV Reverse angle president salutes as men march past	29 sec.	and taken his family out of the country just in
	32 sec.	time.

One of the best tips about scripting good pictures is—don't. The greater the action, the greater the need to say less. The same principle applies to good sound: *let* the band play, the chanting be heard, the shots ring out. When words are needed in quantity it is important to use them to their best advantage. Too many inexperienced writers use up all their most interesting facts to cover the early shots of the film and leave themselves short of anything else to say at the end. Even the commentary to cover a routine, 30 sec. item, instead of being allowed to dribble weakly to a conclusion, can be structured to ensure a proper opening, middle and end.

Building in the pauses

As has already been made clear, the shot-list is the only sure method by which the writer is able to identify specific moments in an edited newsfilm with any real accuracy.

If the three words a second formula is applied to the example on page 72 it would take 54 words to reach the beginning of the shot where the party leader emerges from his car. But this does not allow for the fact that there may be some good 'natural' sound to be heard, that the writer may not wish to cover all 18 sec. with commentary or, indeed, that there may not be enough to say that is relevant.

Added to all that is the possibility that hesitation or a 'fluff' may make the reader's speed vary, so that by the time 18 sec. have elapsed he may be significantly out of step with the pictures. What is needed, therefore, is some measure of control over the reader during the film's transmission.

Imagine that the edited film in the following example is a variation on The Party Leader Arrives. This time it is the foreign minister of a friendly country. He is about to conclude a big trade deal which includes the sale of military equipment. Outside the building where the signing ceremony is to take place, police struggle to hold back a group of demonstrators waving banners and repeatedly shouting "Butter not guns!" As he arrives the minister ignores the crowd and goes straight in to his meeting:

Shot-list

General view minister's car and escort	.... 3 sec.
Medium shot ring of police linking arms to restrain crowd	.... 7 sec.
Closeup minister out of car, waving	....11 sec.
Medium shot group with banners chanting "Butter not guns!"	....16 sec.
Minister walks straight past, up stairs into building	....22 sec.

Consulting this shot-list back in the newsroom, the writer decides that the most interesting point is the brief confrontation between demonstrators and politician, and that the chants of "Butter not guns!" should be heard without the accompanying distraction of the newsreader's voice. The aim, then, is to hold the reader back for the five seconds of the chanting and then to give a signal to restart the commentary immediately afterwards.

The secret lies in part in the layout of the written script on the newsreader's desk. As the film is transmitted the reader speaks the commentary until the point is reached where the word *cue* appears in the left-hand margin. This is the signal to treat the *preceding* full stop as an invisible barrier which must not be passed until a signal, probably a coloured light out of the sight of the camera, is given to carry on. The gap between the two may be a few seconds or considerably longer, but the reader must wait for the signal, however long it is in arriving.

Usually the word *cue* is accompanied by a definite time, to indicate when the reader is to be signalled to restart the commentary. More often than not it is the scriptwriter who does the cueing, using the film leader countdown from the control gallery as a guide for starting a stop watch.

"As the Minister arrived, large numbers of police were kept busy holding back groups of left-wing demonstrators determined to make it known what *they* thought of the arms deal."

In this case the reader will have reached the words ". . . thought of the arms deal" in exactly 10 seconds. Seeing the instruction "Cue 16 seconds" he pauses. At 11 seconds the film reaches the point where demonstrators begin chanting. As the second hand on the watch reaches 16, the writer presses the button operating the cue light and the reader smoothly picks up the thread of the commentary:

"But even if he heard them the minister didn't appear to notice the protests".

For sheer professional results, the stopwatch and cue light method is difficult to beat, despite the danger that in occasional moments of stress the scriptwriter is likely to press the wrong button and stop the watch too soon. Nevertheless, it is generally recognised that only the writer knows intimately what the film contains and is in a position to make minor adjustments to cue times, even during transmission. In any case, most writers are obsessively protective towards their precious film scripts and are uneasy about leaving them in the care of anyone else.

Where there are no arrangements for cue lights to be worked by editorial staff, the operation is usually carried out from the control gallery by the production secretary, although this would appear to be putting an unfair additional burden on someone already well occupied with duties during transmission.

Hand signals relayed by the floor manager on instruction from the gallery seem likely to increase the time-lag between cue and newsreader reaction. The same objection may be made about a system where the newsreader is expected to pick up his own cues from the monitor at some recognisable point in the film. This invariably means waiting for a shot-change, and by the time the reader has reacted, the viewer may have spent two, and maybe three seconds looking at some new, unexplained scene.

From the reader's point of view, too, it is unsatisfactory, as it is all too easy to fall behind if the script is tightly written. This self-cueing system should be discouraged almost as much as the one where the poor newsreader is given such imprecise written instructions as 'pause for three seconds', and is then expected to hit every shot with unfailing accuracy.

Of course, every reader needs some time to react, whatever cueing system is employed, and in planning the script it is essential that the writer builds in a nominal one second between every cue and the expected resumption of commentary. Experience will tell whether that is long enough.

Writers vary in the way they set out to construct their scripts, but the method favoured by many is to begin by writing the words around one key shot, not always at the start of the film, and then building up the commentary before and after it, fitting in the cues as necessary. At this stage, unless pressure of time is great, it is wise to put more or less anything down on paper, leaving any 'polishing' of words and phrases until the first draft is complete. This method is further helped by writing only three words to a line, preferably on a ruled pad, so making it simple to add up the number of seconds of commentary already written. It is surprisingly easy to lose count if the words for a 40 second script are strung out across the page, and minor adjustments may take far longer than expected.

Accurate identification of shots can be achieved with consistency *only as a result of careful writing and cueing from the shot-list*. 'Block' scripts, those written over the entire length of film without pause, should be reserved for those infrequent occasions where specific identification is not necessary. It is also leaving too much to chance to allow more than 20 seconds without a cue . . . far less when individuals need accurate identification.

At the other extreme lies the temptation to insert a cue for every sentence of script. This soon becomes boring and predictable: the aim should be a reasonable variation in the length of cues so that sometimes a single paragraph straddles a sequence of shots. If necessary it may mean padding out when there is too little to say, cutting out words when there is too much, or even achieving balance by 'borrowing' a phrase from one shot to say over another. In that way, one neatly-constructed sentence, cued to coincide with, say, the first in a series of ministerial arrivals, should ensure perfect synchronism between words and pictures.

Finally, if things do go awry, it is far better that the script should anticipate what is about to happen rather than follow what has already taken place. The viewer ought never to be left in in limbo, staring at a brand new shot and wondering for a few uncomfortable moments whether he is being prevented from hearing the commentary because something has gone wrong with the television set.

Cueing into filmed speech

Some of the problems involved in cueing sound effects within a film have already been touched on. A whole new set of circumstances present themselves when the sound is that of human speech.

Much of what is spoken on television newsfilm emanates from two categories of people, namely reporters or those being interviewed by reporters. In either case, the aim of the newswriter must be to construct any additional commentary for transmission in a way which links most naturally into the words already recorded on the sound track.

Where this comes within the body of the film rather than at the beginning, the onus rests even more heavily on the editorial staff to ensure that the speech arrives a decent breath's pause after the commentary introducing it. Failure results in either an embarrassing, over-long delay between the two, or worse, what in the US is called 'upcutting', the ugly overlap of live commentary and recorded sound.

Accuracy is achieved fairly easily, by positioning a cue paragraph immediately before the sound extract. The actual wording itself is also of enormous importance, and the writer is taking unnecessary risks if a planned lead-in to speech demands timing to the split second.

> "Reporting on the latest round of pay talks, the general secretary told the conference"
> (General secretary speaks)

will be impressive if the sound is heard without delay, but

> "The general secretary reported on the latest round of pay talks"
> (General secretary speaks)

would be much safer, for it would still make sense if the speech on film were delayed for a few seconds or did not arrive at all through some technical fault.

The whole principle is based on the fact that flexibility rests with the writer's words and not on the speech placed at an immovable point on the film sound track.

With interviews in which the reporter's first or only question has been edited out, the words leading up to the answer must be carefully phrased to produce a response which matches, otherwise there is a clear danger that the writer will be guilty of putting words into the interviewee's mouth. It is equally important to remember that if the viewer is about to be shown a filmed close-up of a question being answered, the preceding commentary should leave no doubt about who is to speak. This is best achieved by referring to the first speaker *last*.

So it is:

> "Tom Bailey asked the Prime Minister for his reaction"
> (Prime Minister answers)

rather than

> "The Prime Minister talked to Tom Bailey"
> (Prime Minister answers)

Vision introductions to filmed reports should follow similar principles.

> "We've just received this report from Tom Bailey"

ought to have Our Man visible or audible at once. The introduction which ends lamely with the words

> "Our Bogshire newsroom reports"

suggests a scene of newsroomers busily at work, and the viewer is likely to be rather puzzled if the opening shot shows, instead, an exterior dominated by an un-named reporter. In any event the flat statement

> "Our Bogshire newsroom reports"

makes listening which, by any standards, is less than riveting. Far more worthwhile is an introduction which actually passes on some information at the same time as preparing the viewer for what is coming next:

> "Tom Bailey has been finding out why exports have suddenly fallen off"

has, at least, the merit of suggesting to the viewer that it might be worth keeping awake to watch the film report about to follow.

Selecting sound extracts

The selection of one or more extracts from a lengthy filmed interview obviously depends on the amount of space the item has been allocated within a news programme. As it is fairly unusual for any interview to be shot to its exactly prescribed duration, however experienced the principals taking part, a certain amount of choice will inevitably be necessary. Given time, the programme editor may wish to make this a personal choice but, just as frequently, it will be the newsroom-based scriptwriter who is faced with the task.

As every interview is unique, it is impossible to set down rigid rules. On some occasions the single one-minute answer out of six will stand out. On others, the reporter concerned may have strong views about the merits of a particular section and offer guidance. The firmest general guideline probably goes no further than a suggestion that the ultimate value of any news interview rests in the opinion and interpretation of facts by the subject being interviewed. The facts themselves are best left for the writer to assemble as part of the newsreader's introduction.

In making the choice, the newswriter also needs to be aware that much more is involved than suitability of duration and content. The physical cutting into, or out of, any filmed speech at precisely the required point *editorially* may, at the same time, not be feasible *technically*. So even at the expense of a few extra, unwanted seconds of screen time, the aim should always be to cut at the most natural points, ends of answers or, where the selection consists of only part of a sound passage, a stop or breath pause during which inflection of the voice is downwards.

Although most people are well aware that editing takes place it is always much better to avoid any cut which will appear both ugly and obvious.

Temptations to avoid

Puns . . .

Experienced writers usually consider that a really important, well-shot newsfilm story virtually tells itself, the task becoming one of assembling facts in an order dictated by the quality and sequence of the pictures. Much more testing are the down-bulletin film items, often weekend fillers, for which little information is readily available.

With these 'soft' stories, the temptation is for the writer to produce a stream of glib generalities or a series of puns, the aim in either case presumably being to lower a verbal curtain through which the lack of facts will not be noticed. There are occasions when this approach might work. But, for example, a balloon race film which wrings out such lines as 'soaring reputations' or 'rising hopes' will, all too quickly, have the viewer reaching for the 'Off' switch in disgust.

. . . and clichés.

For any unwary writer, the cliché presents another booby trap, and in television news it is a double-edged one at that, since trite pictures are just as likely to find their way on to the air as are trite phrases. Probably every viewer of every television news programme in the world has had to suffer his own local equivalent of the following British examples of the film cliché:

> Trade union leaders arriving for or leaving from talks about pay.

> The Chancellor of the Exchequer holding aloft the despatch box containing secrets of the annual budget.

> Government ministers filing through the open door of Number 10, Downing Street for a crisis Cabinet meeting with the Prime Minister.

> Any VIP descending any aircraft steps anywhere.

> Shots of camera crews filming or security men on rooftops, used to telescope the action between aircraft steps and official car.

As for the words, it seems almost impossible for some writers to avoid trotting out the stock phrase to satisfy the stock situation:

The Major Fire
"Fifty/a hundred firemen fought/battled the blaze/flames"
"Smoke could be seen five/ten/fifty miles away"
"Firemen rushed . . ."

The Air Disaster
"Wreckage was scattered over a wide area"
"Rescuers tore at the wreckage with their bare hands"

The Great Escape
"Police with tracker dogs combed the area"
"A massive manhunt/search has begun"
"Road blocks have been set up"

The VIP Visit
"Security was strict/tight"

The Holiday Snarl-up
"Traffic was bumper-to-bumper"

Almost Any Story
"Earlier"
"Later"
"Meanwhile"
"Today"

and that is not to forget my own personal favourite, usually attributed to a middle-aged eye-witness to any violent incident in the south of England:

"It was just like the Blitz".

To be fair, it is perfectly understandable that when time is short and the pressure great, it is the familiar line rather than the elegant phrase which will suggest itself to the newswriter. In any case, the overriding consideration must always be to get the commentary on the air, however lacking in originality.

But that ought to be reserved for the last resort. Where second thoughts are possible, the tired old standby must be shunned. As it was most appositely put by Fred Holtum, a senior writer for BBC TV News in London, during a serious discussion of the subject:

"Avoid clichés . . . like the plague".

Working with videotape

Many a newsfilm which begins its short life in the 16mm sound camera ultimately ends it on the screen as a videotape recording (VTR). For the major TV news services involved in network programming the chief advantage is the obvious one of speed. Where processing, editing and telecine facilities are available locally, it is much quicker to send the result electronically along a public telecommunications cable to programme headquarters than physically by plane or train.

Anything photographed by the electronic television camera in the studio or outside may also be linked to VT and prepared for replaying in no greater time than it takes to rewind the tape.

Coupled with the strides made in intercontinental communications systems, the development of videotape has added a new dimension to the business of gathering foreign news in particular. The whole effect has been to extend news deadlines right up until the ends of programmes, providing editors with a flexibility previously unknown.

Not that the desirability of recording pictures for television is in any way new. The whole range of hazards connected with transmitting almost anything 'live' was recognised long ago, even before the introduction of the first methods of filming programmes or segments off high-quality television monitors. Despite their success, these systems had to rely on the conventional photographic techniques of processing and editing, with inevitable delays before the recordings could be examined.

The major snag in developing instant visual playback capabilities along the lines of $\frac{1}{4}$ in tape sound recordings lay in the very high speed needed and consequent amount of tape expended to reproduce pictures of sufficiently high quality. Eventually, in the late fifties, the race was won in the United States by the Ampex company, which invented a machine to tackle the problem from a different direction. This involved keeping the speed of a two-inch (51 mm) wide magnetic tape down to 15 inches (38 cm) a second as it was moved past four recording heads rotating about a hundred times faster.

The result of this 'quadruplex' technique was picture reproduction which most laymen found indistinguishable from the original, and for the name of Ampex a special place in the language of television.

Since then, the high capital outlay involved in the purchase and installation of the latest generation of colour videotape machines has encouraged the television organisations to seek broadcast quality at less expense. Substantial progress has been made with systems of helical scanning across half or one-inch tape by fewer heads.

To look at, the conventional quadruplex of whatever make resembles an overgrown, complicated version of the familiar reel-to-reel tape recorder (Fig. 24). Each videotape machine and its ancillary equipment occupies a space about the size of a small room, and is operated by a trained engineer. The tape itself is wound on to spools which run for about 90 minutes, and an integral counter helps the operator to keep track of individual recordings, some of which may last for no more than a few seconds. Fast rewinding, from the extreme end of the tape, takes about five minutes. Recordings may be erased and the same tape used over and over again without loss of quality until 'pile-up',

VIDEOTAPE RECORDING

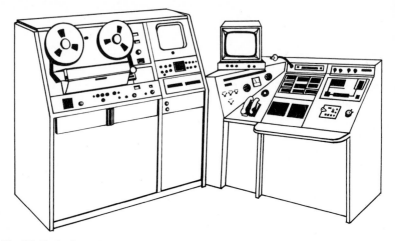

Fig. 24. Typical quadruplex videotape recorder. Two inch wide tape runs for 90 min and has a life of many hours. Editing is achieved electronically, using a pair of machines.

thick, horizontal lines of interference, shows that its useful life is at an end.

As an individual machine in a busy news organisation may make several recordings each day, there is a definite routine which has to be observed on every occasion. Where the recording is made from an outside source nothing is possible without the advance booking (in the UK) of Post Office telecommunication circuits between sending and receiving points. Decisions about recording times are frequently based on editorial guesswork concerning film still to be shot about news events yet to take place.

At the appointed time, sound and vision links are established through a central control point, which also enables the engineers at each end to communicate direct. Having carried out a series of checks to test the circuits and assuming that the material to be sent is ready, they agree a mutually convenient moment for the transfer to begin, allowing long enough for the machinery to stabilise at its correct operating speed.

Once transmission is complete, the receiving engineer checks the recording for quality by replaying it from beginning to end, although with particularly lengthy or very late items only random spot-checks may be possible. Once satisfied, the receiving engineer informs the sender and tells central control that the recording is finished and the circuits are no longer required. Where something has gone wrong, a decision must be made about a re-run of the material, provided enough of the booked time remains.

Editing a videotape recording

By far the most significant development in the videotape operation of recent years has been the improvement in the speed and quality of editing. At first this was a slow process requiring physical cutting and joining after literally microscopic examination of the magnetic surface.

Besides taking approximately fifteen minutes to accomplish, each physical edit also ruined that particular portion of tape. This laborious method has now been made virtually obsolete by the technique of 'invisible' electronic editing, which leaves the tape unimpaired and, in expert hands, is extremely fast. Two machines are required, as the chosen sections from the original are played from one to another which re-records them in sequence until a complete cut-story is obtained. Accuracy of editing is achieved to the split second by the use of an intricate device which in one system allows a blip tone to be recorded on to the cue track (the secondary of the two sound tracks on the tape), so identifying each editing point.

Edits can be made in sound or vision only, and sound from other sources, such as reporters' telephoned commentaries, can be transferred from ordinary $\frac{1}{4}$in tape for synchronising with the pictures.

If film editing is an art, then VT editing becomes a science when practised by skilful engineers capable of achieving a coherent pictorial precis from many hours of recorded material. So adept have they become at this electronic wizardry, videotape engineers in general sometimes share criticism with producers for helping to create action and interest out of events, particularly sport, which, in reality, were fairly lifeless and uninteresting. As far as news is concerned, there *are* circumstances in which too smooth an edit would create the wrong impression, and it would be more ethical to make the cut in a way which deliberately avoids giving the impression that the action or speech is continuous.

The greater the volume of material, the greater the difficulty in making editorial judgements about content. A newswriter may spend a whole day in the videotape department watching an important state occasion or some sporting event like a cricket test match and then be expected to condense the contents of five or six full tapes into a maximum two minutes' air time.

The secret lies in the methodical, accurate logging of events as they occur and, wherever possible, the building up of an edited story during the longest natural breaks in action. This is sometimes inclined to force writers into making hasty and occasionally wrong decisions about what to include. But it remains the lesser of two evils. Even the most expert and willing VT operator would be hard pressed to make a swift compilation of half a dozen incidents spread over an equal number of tapes, since loading and unloading can be a time-consuming business.

On occasion, the recording may be of a major event being broadcast simultaneously by another part of the television organisation, and the newswriter may be asked to stipulate whether it is proposed to use the accompanying commentary or merely the natural sound effects when an edited version is transmitted for news purposes.

The one question to be answered here is whether a commentary recorded at the time would inhibit the choice of pictorial edits made at a later stage. The usual answer will be 'yes', for the combination of picture, commentary sound and natural sound is technically impossible to unravel. Therefore the newswriter should invariably settle for the 'clean' sound, obtained by bypassing the sound circuit carrying the commentary. But this can still be recorded on to the cue track for guidance and, if necessary, can be transferred to the edited version later on.

How to write to videotape

Of the few genuine problems which affect the journalist writing to videotape, the most obvious is the technical limitation in all but the very latest machines which prevents the tape from continuing to reproduce sound or pictures when it is stopped, unlike film where the pictures can be halted at a precise frame.

This in no way restricts editing techniques. But it does make a hazardous, hit-or-miss affair out of most shot-listing which, as in film, provides the whole basis for accurate scripting. Despite some advances in electronic time-keeping methods, the best solution remains for the writer to be equipped with a stop-watch and to be well positioned to watch the item as it is recorded. A rough shot-list can be made at that time and during the replay check which follows. One more viewing only may then be necessary as confirmation. Although there is no deterioration in the quality of a recording after several further replays, lack of time may prevent the engineer running it through again for the sake of the writer. After the shot-list has been completed, writing goes ahead on the established principle of three words to the second.

With one relatively minor difference, introductions to video-taped items should be treated in the same way as those for film. Enough introductory words need to be written to cover the period, usually ten seconds,[1] it takes for the machine to reach the speed at which the picture is held steady. It makes it that much more difficult for the studio director to cue in the tape at the required moment if it becomes necessary to calculate some of the thirty-word run-up time from the end of the commentary for a preceding news item.

Cueing methods

While conventional stop-watch/light cueing methods may be applied with equal success to videotape, one extra difficulty arises out of any editorial choice of a section some way in from the start of a recording. This problem is not so apparent where silent or effects-only film is concerned, for the writer and engineer will usually find guidance in the position of shot-changes. Starting from the spot selected as the opening, the engineer spools the tape *backwards* for ten seconds, at which point the electronic 'blip' is applied or the tape surface marked with a chinagraph pencil. In this way the operator is certain to hit the correct opening shot every time the standard 10-second cue is given from the control gallery.

To ensure similar accuracy with *speech*, the newswriter needs to provide even more information for the studio director, the aim being to introduce the chosen words at the correct moment, not mistakenly early, late, or in the middle of a sentence. To this end, some television news organisations insist that writers mark their written scripts with what is known as a 'pre-hear' cue, the final few unwanted words immediately preceding those which *are* required. Suppose, in the example

Q: What's the government's next move?

A: Well . . . um . . . let me see . . . er . . . I suppose that what we'll have to do is to . . .

---

[1]Telecine run-up time is usually anywhere between three and ten seconds, depending on the type of machine. For film *or* VT Studio Directors add an extra second for their own purposes.

the decision is taken to omit the question and transmit only that part of the interview beginning "I suppose", the pre-hear cue will consist of probably the whole of the question and the opening words of the answer, up to and including the second 'fluff'. So, on paper, it would appear as

> Pre-hear cue: "What's the government's next move? Well... um . . . let me see . . . er" (pause)

> Sound begins: "I suppose that . . ."

On transmission, the control gallery staff would be listening carefully, consulting their scripts at the same time, ready to bring up the sound on tape at the end of the ten-second run-up, at the moment the interviewee is about to say the words "I suppose".

One last point is worth making about videotape. Faced with the somewhat overpowering technology and strange jargon which surrounds this particular area of television news, many a newcomer to newswriting is understandably apprehensive. All the same, it need not take too long to appreciate that, for all its apparent complications, videotape is just another tool, and is quite capable of being mastered.

The sure way is to turn to the engineers, who will react sympathetically to any request for help or explanation. They are, after all, members of the same team.

Last words about pictures

Writing to moving pictures presents the newswriter with a genuine opportunity to extend journalistic experience into a completely new area. Yet, paradoxically, it remains one with limits which some regard as too restrictive. In accepting the first principle that there can be no place for scripted words totally unrelated to the pictures accompanying them, the newswriter may feel that a straitjacket is being fashioned from the very material it was believed would lead the viewer to new heights of understanding.

Among some professional newswriters this feeling is sincere, the gap seemingly unbridgeable. It need not be, provided what is an apparent weakness in the whole foundation of TV news is seen as a means of refining news senses to the point where every single word is carefully chosen before being put to work.

As confidence improves, the dedicated convert to television news discovers that within the boundaries of content and dura-

90

tion, the treatment of words and pictures as complementary in character makes it possible to convey deeper understanding of both.

To begin moving towards that goal the writer must take time and care in applying, ultimately by instinct, what can only be described as the Golden Rules of News Scriptwriting:

1. Words and pictures must go together.

2. The commentary must not repeat in detail what viewers are able to see and hear for themselves.

3. The commentary must not describe in detail what viewers are *not able* to see or hear for themselves.

4. The commentary must not be over-written. Or to put it another way, the best script is often the one with the fewest words.

TELEVISION NEWS REPORTING

The glamour of the road

DESPITE the enormous satisfaction it is quite possible to derive from the business of putting together complicated news stories for transmission in a very short time, there is not much doubt that the glamour image of the average newsroom journalist lags far behind that of those who appear in front of the camera. For while no viewer would be expected to be able to name any member of the back-room team, descriptions of nationally-known news performers, the 'Talent', as the Americans quaintly describe them, trip easily off the tongue.

So it is hardly surprising that, sooner or later, many a starry-eyed newcomer to television news begins itching to achieve what is believed to be the ideal—to be seen by an audience of millions through a film report made in some exotic, relatively troubled spot the other side of the globe.

That is probably a perfect example of what might be called the greener-grass syndrome, for there are certainly some reporters who would dearly love to exchange their peripatetic lives for what they regard as the calmer existence of those pulling the strings from their desks in the newsroom. Even experienced television reporters privately admit that, after a while, the apparent glamour and excitement of their lives begin to pall. Some, sooner than others, learn to detest rushing to catch planes or deadlines, living out of suitcases, eating hurried meals in unhygienic places abroad, witnessing at first hand unspeakable horrors of which the wider audience may ultimately see very little.

All this in addition to the real personal dangers involved in covering the stuff of modern television news, wars, natural disasters, civil unrest. That professional newsmen doing their job are just as much at risk as the combatants has been proved time and again by recent events in Vietnam, Cambodia, Cyprus and the Middle East.

Many reporters are married with family responsibilities, and live with the uneasy feeling that any birthday party, wedding anniversary or other normal domestic occasion may be interrupted by a sudden telephone call commanding them to be on the next flight to somewhere or other. The wife of one former TV news general reporter used to maintain that the one thing which perpetually un-nerved her was the small suitcase, containing spare shirts, underwear and shaving kit, which stood permanently in the hall, as a reminder of the emergency assignment which might come at any time. Understandably, not all marriages endure that sort of strain.

Of course no sensible reporter pretends it is all hectic. Most will readily recall hours wasted at airports, in draughty corridors of government or other buildings, waiting for events to take place or people turn up. Sometimes they did not. At other times, doors slammed, telephones went dead, the answer was 'no comment' or something less polite.

In contrast there are pleasant, well-ordered and interesting assignments, at which the reporter is greeted with enthusiasm, hospitality and a genuine invitation to call again.

The result of a job well done may be two or three minutes of good film, a visual by-line and an enhanced reputation, yet the dominating factor of it all is that the reporter cannot work alone is the assignment is to be carried out properly. For while the solo newspaperman and the radio reporter in the field are as close to the office as the nearest telephone, the television news reporter has to work with a film camera crew, an outside broadcast unit, or a television studio linked in some way with home base.

Even in these days of compact, mobile equipment, this is bound to put the television news reporter at a distinct disadvantage when it comes to the scrimmages which are frequently part and parcel of world news-gathering. There is little point in pushing through a crowd of other equally eager newsmen, only to discover that one or both members of the film crew have been left behind struggling with their gear.

Yet to be effective, the TV reporter cannot be content to hover aloof on the fringe of a story in the hope of eventually being granted special dispensation by the other participants. Despite the fact that the obtrusiveness of the camera, sound equipment and lights makes the entire team the target for attention and occasional abuse, any reporter who is not up with the herd, and sometimes in front of it, does not last very long.

93

Ironically, perseverence and initiative at times work to the reporter's own detriment. How often it seems that the fruits of a good TV interview, grabbed against all odds, are picked up by other newsmen in the crowd and, with minimal embellishment, are turned into highly acceptable accounts for their own branches of the news business.

In the end though, the reporter for TV news is only as effective as his last film report. There is no glory to be won from the production of a brilliant piece of work which arrives home too late to be processed and edited in time for transmission. Time, effort and money are all wasted if, at the conclusion of some expensive foreign mission, the film is impounded by customs.

Few television reporters begin their careers as such. Most graduate from newspapers, news agencies or radio, and so lack only the knowledge of television techniques to become successful.

Leaving aside the matter of journalistic ability, a modicum of which must be assumed, the TV reporter's two most basic qualities necessary before being let loose in front of an unsuspecting viewing public would seem to be a reasonably personable appearance and clear diction.

In Britain, ideas have undoubtedly changed about what constitutes diction good enough for broadcasting. For the general increase in news outlets, particularly since the coming of local radio in 1967, has allowed all manner of accents and speech impediments to become suddenly more acceptable. Whether this is interpreted as a lowering of standards or a welcome move towards more genuine spoken English is a matter for individual opinion. However, the cruel truth about television is that some patently expert journalists simply lack credibility as performers on film or in the studio, and that the most carefully-researched, well-written material is totally lost to the nine-tenths of an audience fascinated instead by a nervous tic, bobbing Adam's apple or inability to keep the head straight.

Not only that. What some viewers consider to be incorrect pronunciation is guaranteed to induce near apoplexy on the part of the critics, amateur and professional alike. During 1974 and early 1975, Bernard Levin of the London *Times* devoted hundreds of words to reprimanding certain broadcasters, TV news reporters among them, for sometimes pronouncing the word 'thee' instead of 'the'.

To the uncaring, it may have been much ado about nothing. Yet Mr Levin was undeniably correct in his assessment of the *result*, that "the ugly, flat, distorted and meaningless noises made by the chief sinners are so boring that they have the inevitable effect of making the listener's attention wander, though they may be telling us of important things we need to know".[1]

Still, at least such misdemeanours are capable of being cured, unlike the expressionless monotones and nasal whines which apparently defy the best efforts of the voice-coachers.

Little can be done either it seems for those with voices so light and high-pitched as to make virtually no impact for broadcasting. Women figure largely among the sufferers, which may account in part for what some interpret as discrimination against female journalists in TV news, although the million-dollar wooing of Barbara Walters from one American network to another and the inclusion of Angela Rippon in the BBC's *Nine O'Clock News* team of newsreaders, may help give the lie to that notion.

Another, more cynical theory about women television journalists is that male viewers might spend all their time nursing lewd thoughts about a really attractive girl reporter during her appearances on the box while other females among the audience either hate her on principle or wonder where she is coiffeured. Either way, all is lost.

For these reasons, chocolate-box good looks and speech which is too precise are considered equally off-putting whether found in men or women. Among all save those who mourn the demise of the Hollywood glamour factories, the preference is for people who at least look and sound as though they lead real lives off screen.

All this merely goes to emphasise how easy it is to be critical. Given the curious chemistry at work in everybody's likes and dislikes, it is interesting to speculate the result of a computer programmed to produce an identikit picture of the reporter most likely to win universal appeal.

Without the benefit of the computer, it must all be down to intelligent guesswork and a single, old-fashioned word—style.

Learning the ropes
The novice reporter discovers quickly enough that there is no short cut on the tortuous route which may eventually lead to general acceptance as a competent television performer. There is likely to be very little in the way of formal 'coaching', as the

---

[1] *The Times*, January 29, 1975.

average news service seems to expect its newcomers to pick up as they go along everything except the absolute basics. This is sometimes euphemistically described as 'on-the-job training'.

Once some initial progress has been made, usually after a few painful lessons on the way, the new reporter may be taken aside by a more senior colleague and told gently about some of the most apparent flaws in his performance. Some of these might be avoided in the first place by the expenditure of a relatively small amount of time on three major factors:

1. Speech
Each reporter ultimately develops a natural, personal style of delivery and emphasis, and although this individuality is to be encouraged, the aim in every case must be clarity, with delivery at an even pace. It must be neither slow enough to be irritating, nor fast enough for the words to run into each other. As part of a general tendency to group words and phrases in a manner which sounds odd as well as ungrammatical, one of the most frequent faults is the addition of non-existent full stops in the middle of sentences. The cure could not be more simple: sentences which are too long should be broken up into shorter ones. Oral stumbles (fluffs) and hesitations inevitably marr otherwise fluent performances and perhaps lead to loss of confidence. The answer is for the reporter to become familiar with the contents of the script by rehearsing as thoroughly as possible (mumbling in a corner, though a poor substitute, is better than nothing). But when serious mistakes *do* occur there is no shame in asking for a second 'take' where film or videotape is concerned. Even the most experienced performers expect to trip over their words from time to time. Where any faults persist, there is no harm in seeking the advice of speech therapists, who are able to devise little training programmes for the tongue in a way which can only increase the performer's confidence.

2. Mannerisms
In reporters with easygoing, relaxed personalities, tiny mannerisms may even become endearing to the viewer. An occasional frown, raising of the eyebrows or head movement to emphasise a point probably comes across as genuine involvement in the story at hand. For the rest, stiff, awkward movements, facial contortions and continual passing of

tongue between dry lips are among the many tell-tale signs of stage-fright. Usually, this passes once confidence comes, although not always. I know of one former reporter who, while totally relaxed in the atmosphere of the radio studio, betrayed his nerves during appearances on television by prefacing almost every sentence with the word 'well', even though he knew it did not appear once in the script he had written. Nervousness is not equally shared between film and studio performances, for in many ways the electronic camera seems to magnify mannerisms which, to the consternation of the studio staff, reveal themselves only under the strain of live transmission. Some reporters slouch back in their chairs, others tilt like the Leaning Tower, or hunch their bodies so that one shoulder is thrust forward aggressively across the desk. Possibly worst of all is the fear which has the reporter sitting literally on the seat edge. The result is a close resemblance to the jockey on horseback, except that to the hapless viewer the rider here seems poised to leap through the screen and land in the front room. To all those who suffer from it, stage-fright (no respecter of persons) is an awful thing, for which there is no panacea. Practice, however painful, will make a difference, particularly if backed up by the close scrutiny of film or videotape recordings of personal performances. The advice of production staff, given and accepted in the right spirit, will also help the novice to isolate and then dispose of the main problems which, if left to develop, might lead to permanent bad habits.

3. Dress
The medium itself imposes some restrictions on dress; the sensitive mechanism inside electronic colour cameras seems unable to digest certain striped or checked patterns which create disturbing visual hiccups known as strobing. Even so, it is no real limitation of personal freedom to require any reporter of either sex to avoid clothes and colours which the majority of viewers would be bound to consider eccentric. Not that reporters are expected to travel everywhere with vast wardrobes capable of meeting all eventualities. All that is expected is reasonable anticipation about the relevance of dress to story. For example, an open-necked bush shirt and denims would be entirely appropriate garb for the coverage of a desert war, while a pin-striped business suit and homburg

would not. Equally, a formal studio interview calls for jacket, collar and tie so long as these remain convention. For women there are enough smart, business-like styles available to preserve femininity without resorting to anything fussy, although almost anything they wear on television seems to be regarded as fair game for criticism. When Angela Rippon began reading the BBC *Nine O'Clock News* regularly her clothes became the subject of national debate, and one newspaper even went so far as to ask leading designers to 'dress' her, superimposing the results over a series of stock pictures. As for grooming, it would be unfair to expect the viewing audience to accept uncombed hair or two days' growth when the reporters' families would not, except in those situations where such appearances are relevant to the story. Beads, jangling bracelets or long earrings are best avoided, as their movements are inclined to create distraction at the wrong moment, particularly should they fall off. Lapel badges, especially those which *just* defy identification, are fraught with danger. So is the whole range of what might be called 'club' ties. The possibility here is that the viewer might miss all that is being said while concentrating hard to see whether the neat insignia three inches below the knot turns out to be of real significance or just a gravy stain.

Reporter's role

In most centrally-run news services, the reporter's duties are fairly clear-cut, with daily on-location assignments carried out on the instruction of programme editors or the semi-independent machinery created to run newsgathering operations.

A certain amount of briefiing is usually given, even if limited to the approximate outline any contribution is expected to follow to enable it to take its place within the rest of the day's programme. Where an assignment is foreseen as representing only one segment of wider coverage of a single topic, briefing is much more detailed. Good preparation is vital in any case. Given reasonable warning of the nature of the assignments, most diligent reporters make a virtual fetish out of 'reading themselves in' from any available background material. On foreign assignments this may run to dossiers built up from previous visits and include a diversity of facts ranging in importance from currency exchange rates down to the names and localities of reliable laundries.

Travel arrangements vary. To ensure speed off the mark,

those news services able to afford it provide individual reporters with office cars, complete with two-way radio telephone links, or at least contribute fuel costs towards the reporter's own transport. For those unwilling or unable to tie up large amounts of capital in fleets of cars, reporters are expected to travel with the technical crews or simply jump in taxis, either paying as they go and recouping the money later or, as part of official arrangements with taxi companies, signing the driver's log at the end of each journey.

Some news services operate a pool transport system to ferry all operational staff to and from assignments, but this has its drawbacks. There are apocryphal tales of news teams stranded miles out of town at headquarters, officially unable to move until an office car became available, while some government building burnt to the ground.

Once on location, technical matters are clearly the business of the film crew but, except on those occasions where the unit is accompanied by a 'fixer' (see page 155), it is the reporter who has to shoulder the 'managerial' mantle, with overall responsibility for the shape and content of coverage.

In between lies a fascinating, ill-defined area of ground which, in *non*-news film work, would be covered by a director. For reasons chiefly of cost and mobility, it is generally accepted that television news does not need to have separate directors, the role being shared between reporter and cameraman on the spot. So it is probably here that the greatest scope exists for disagreement among the members of the crew.

The ideal working compromise consists of a reporter with journalistic skills and an eye for pictures sketching an outline to be filled in by a sympathetic, experienced film crew. Detailed discussion about the best way to achieve the desired end product is advisable before a frame of film is exposed. But, in the final analysis, it must be the cameraman who decides what is technically possible to film, according to numerous factors including the available light and distance from the subject.

Once a general storyline has been agreed, the reporter then has to trust the crew to supply what they say they are supplying. Long arguments about the closeness of a close-up or the speed of a pan from left to right only hinder the completion of an assignment, and no professional news cameraman would tolerate a reporter's demand to look through the camera viewfinder before every shot.

Relationships are therefore important, particularly on some dangerous foreign assignments when the degree of mutual trust between members of the team could make all the difference—literally—between life and death. Sometimes a reporter and crew will build up personal friendships and respect over a series of difficult, successfully-completed assignments. Between others the chemistry will be all wrong, and no amount of attempted peace-making will put it right. To team a lazy reporter with a go-getting crew or vice-versa and still expect the screen to reflect only successful results is wishful thinking. Far better to ensure that, where possible, incompatible factions are kept well apart.

Even when prospects for cooperation are good, there is no certain recipe for success. The reporter must always remember to be considerate and tactful in the treatment of his professional colleagues, resisting any attempts by misguided outsiders to create separate categories of 'officer' (reporter) and 'other ranks' (crew). The reporter who allowed himself to be swept off to the executive dining room while the crew made do in the works canteen would deserve the inevitable opprobrium.

Equally, the film crew must be patient with a nervous or out-of-sorts reporter. After a long, tiring day with very little food or drink, it is often tempting for the cameraman to give the thumbs-up to a reporter's performance he knows deep down to be flawed, just as the timid reporter—suspicious that something *may* be wrong—is prepared to accept a personal second best rather than risk offending the crew by encroaching on meal times. Getting the story right must come first. As one experienced cameraman has put it "If the reporter fails, we all fail."

In addition to the constant awareness of deadlines, there also has to be recognition of the need to be as economical as possible in the use of film, not only for the sake of cost, but also for the reason that the greater the volume of material the longer the time necessary for processing, viewing and editing.

With the assignment completed and the film received at head-quarters, the reporter's role becomes less clear, for one of the main planks of the intake-output system is that it is the editorial staff back at the office who assume the ultimate responsibility for shaping the material for inclusion in the programme. Although the reporter's *guidance* may be sought the theory is that those most closely involved in the creation of items are not the best placed to make objective judgements of their value. This is apart from the possibility that all manner of developments may have taken place which downgrade the original importance of the assignment.

It is at this stage that the strict dichotomy of intake and output begins to seem an expensive luxury for the smaller, less wealthy news services. For them, the solution may lie not in sealing their available editorial talent into separate watertight compartments but in seeking to create genuine all-rounders. Each would be an amalgam of news editor, researcher, scriptwriter and reporter, equally well-versed in the skills of overseeing film and videotape editing and writing studio introductions for themselves to read on transmission.

Reporting techniques

Even when Electronic News Gathering eventually succeeds the 16mm sound film camera as the main means of originating news material, most of the reporting techniques now being used to present items in a fluent way for the television screen will continue to be valid. Then, as now, no reporter will be considered competent without having achieved at least partial mastery of a small selection of basic skills which go beyond any proven journalistic ability in the conventional sense.

These techniques, whether for use on film, videotape, outside broadcast or in the studio, are employed either individually or collectively in every contribution a reporter makes to a programme. Each demands its own careful study and development to a point where it can be put into operation smoothly and with a minimum of delay, to add the same kind of professional gloss to the news report that the actor brings to the play.

Pieces to camera

Of all the skills needed for television news reporting, the *piece to camera* or *stand-upper* is among the most frequently used. Although it is sometimes regarded as old-fashioned (indeed some experienced reporters consider they have failed if they have to resort to it), the piece to camera, which is essentially a vision story on film, remains a sure means of telling a story lucidly.

It has three further advantages: it immediately establishes the reporter's presence on the spot; it is extremely simple to execute, and it is fast enough to be considered a kind of contingency sample, rather like the dust scooped up by the first men on the moon in case they had to return to earth rather hurriedly.

Chiefly because of its speed and the fact that there are sometimes no other pictures to supplement it, the piece to camera is frequently designed as a complete report *by itself*, yet the fact remains that it has considerable value as one ingredient within a more comprehensive film report, being versatile enough to be slotted in at almost any point, not necessarily at opening or closing stages only.

The term itself is largely self-descriptive, being those words which the reporter speaks aloud while looking directly at the camera lens and so, through it, to the viewer at home, as the film is exposed. The fact that the majority of pieces to camera are spoken from a straightforward standing position gives rise to its alternative name as *stand upper*.

The technique itself depends on an ability to write spoken language and remember it word for word when delivering it to the camera. But in some respects what matters more is the choice of location for the operation. For example, there seems little to be gained in travelling thousands of miles and then pointing the camera at the reporter standing in front of some anonymous brick wall. Unless the brick wall is germane, or there are legal problems such as exist in filming within court precincts, the aim should always be to show that the reporter is actually where he says he is. To say proudly that our reporter is there is one thing. To prove it to the viewer is something else.

That does not mean going to inordinate lengths to find a background which is visually exciting yet irrelevant to the story. It should be enough to place the reporter in a spot which is appropriate, interesting, but not too distracting. Even if the welcome which greets the news team is not overwhelming, the piece to camera is capable of being completed within a very few minutes, provided that the camera and sound equipment have been tested and are known to be working properly, and the reporter is ready with the words.

Most pieces to camera are filmed as the reporter stands full-face to the lens. But a balanced picture composition must also be achieved. The effect of putting the reporter to one side of the frame (Figs. 25 & 26) rather than right in the centre is that any action in the background is not completely blotted out and the figure becomes a part of the picture rather than a superimposition on it.

Nevertheless, sensible variations on the theme of full face to the lens are to be welcomed, as long as they do not seem to be too contrived. On occasions, the variation is forced upon the reporter by the situation—sitting in aircraft, cars or trains, crouching

102

Fig. 25. Putting the reporter in the middle of the frame has the effect of masking some of the picture.

Fig. 26. Putting him to one side improves composition, making him seem part of the action, not just a superimposition on it.

Fig. 27. (a) Cameraman frames reporter in medium shot for first chunk of script of about 45 words.

Fig. 27. (b) Cameraman changes to close up for second chunk. Film editor cuts two together to produce one continuous take. Unsightly but effective.

under fire or walking along a road. Among the most telling of recent years was the brief piece delivered by BBC reporter Simon Dring while being driven away for treatment to injuries received in the mine explosion which killed a member of his film crew in Cyprus in August, 1974.

Knowing the words

Much of the apprehension felt by novices about their first pieces to camera is caused by doubts that they will be able to remember their words. Admittedly, this can pose a real problem, for it is a knack achieved more easily by some than others.

Yet not only newcomers to television news reporting are haunted by the possibility that even a short, apparently simple piece will require several attempts, resulting in a waste of time, temper and film. Some experienced newsmen admit that, even under the least difficult circumstances, they are unable to remember more than a few words at a time. Others get them right at the first attempt or never. The majority have occasional off-days but generally survive the ordeal without too much trouble.

There is no infallible formula, certainly not ad-libbing, which is inclined to come across as uncertainty rather than spontaneity. Perhaps the only answer is for the beginner to keep the length of commentary down to the maximum capable of being remembered without difficulty. Little is worse than watching someone totter to within the final few sentences of a piece clearly too long to memorise.

While there is no way of avoiding the problem posed by the limits of memory, two possible escape routes suggest themselves. Both are relatively ugly to look at and are therefore strictly second best, but, in a tight corner, are preferable to a halting performance which seems likely to come to a full stop at any moment.

For *Escape No. 1* the reporter needs to ensure that the opening paragraph at least is word-perfect. The rest may then be read from a note-book or clip-board which is clearly in shot so that the viewer is not left wondering how the memory is being refreshed. Subsequent raising of the head from written script towards camera for a sentence or two at a time may add just enough refinement to make the performance tolerable.

Escape No. 2 (Fig. 27a/27b) requires even more than usual co-operation with the cameraman. Here the reporter does not attempt to speak the lines in one continuous take. Instead, the script is learned and then filmed in two separate chunks of, say, 15 seconds, forty five words. For the sections, filmed possibly several minutes apart, then to fit neatly when edited together the two shots of the reporter must be framed in a sufficiently different way to avoid an awkward jump in the middle. The use of this technique should give the reporter enough confidence early on. Later, attempts should be made to train the memory to accept longer and longer pieces, so that eventually there is no need for the split.

Finally, when all is said and done, there is no point in any piece to camera script which fails to refer, even obliquely, to what is going on in the two-thirds of the picture left vacant by the reporter. Where the background is general rather than specific, it is essential that script and location are tied together as firmly as possible, preferably by the opening words, however fragile the real connection between the two.

Studio spots

If the piece to camera is a kind of vision story on film, the *studio spot* is one definition applied to a vision story read in the studio by someone other than a programme's main presenter or newsreader. Usually it is a specialist correspondent or reporter who is called upon to draw together the elements of a particular news story and tell it to the electronic camera in the studio, sometimes with the aid of film or other visual material.

For many reporters these appearances exacerbate the underlying nervousness already discussed, largely because of an awareness that such performances are invariably 'live' ones made in the context of a complete programme, and that the smallest mistakes are therefore incapable of being corrected.

That said, there are considerable advantages for those making studio appearances. First, the script can be prepared up to the time of transmission, making it possible to include the latest information about a 'running' news story. Second, the performance is made in reasonable comfort at a desk in the studio. Third, and probably most important, the reporter may not need to rely on memory for, as well as the written script available out of shot, there will be a device for displaying the words so that the speaker appears to be looking directly at the viewer while reading.

These devices, used by newsreaders in particular, are often referred to by the general term *prompter*. Commonly, the script is copy-typed from the original separate sheets on to a narrow roll of paper which is then fed into a machine and magnified so that the performer is able to read from a distance. The movement of the paper roll is regulated by an operator who has to keep pace as the words are spoken by the reader during transmission.

Some of these machines are free-standing and are placed slightly below or to one side of the camera. The drawback here is that unless placement is perfect the performer may appear to be looking down or away from the viewer.

The Autocue system, as very widely used in television news studios, comes in two parts. One incorporates a tiny television camera which scans the typed prompter roll; the other is a mirror unit mounted on the front of the studio camera. The words are superimposed electronically on the lens photographing the performer, who is then looking straight ahead and reading the script at the same time.

BBC TV news engineers have invented and developed a light-weight portable prompting machine for use in small studios. Here the script can be typed by the reader. One copy is kept for reference, the other fed into a simple projection system which throws the words on to a light cardboard screen set up on a tripod at a suitable point below the camera lens. A further refinement enables the reader to set the machine's speed to match his own personal reading pace, something which can easily be assessed after a short trial run.

A field version, operated by battery, has also been devised. The intention is to make a prompting device as much a part of the reporter's everyday hand-baggage as a notebook and pencil.

All these machines, if used with care, are capable of producing fluent professional performances from almost anyone capable of reading with some expression. It is true that some reporters and programme presenters with prodigious memories consider themselves above using any mechanical aids. But for most, the use of a prompter is infinitely preferable to the alternative—the sight of the top of the head during a performance because constant reference has to be made to a written script on the desk.

Prompting devices are as capable of being misused as any other tool, and many nervous television performers tend to depend on them as lifelines from which they dare not be parted. The frequent result is a near-hypnotic gaze which seems to bore into the viewer.

But the really skilful and experienced user of the machine treats it as a valuable friend and ally, yet is sensible enough not to depend on it entirely. Occasional references to the written script, particularly for figures or other statistics, reassure the viewer that the details are not just being conjured up out of thin air, although by now most members of the public must be aware that no reader could possibly have learned it all.

The prompter script does not contain every single word of a complete news programme. That would take too long to prepare. Instead only the 'vision' extracts are typed out, going usually no further than the first full sentence behind any visual material. From that point onwards the reporter must read from the written page of script. Normally there is a clear indication on the prompter roll so that a natural verbal transition can be achieved from the reader in vision to the illustration:

> page 15:
> The Prime Minister
> arrived in Washington
> shortly after three
> o'clock and went
> straight to the
> White House by
> helicopter
> (vt and script).

The fact that pictures are meant to fill the screen from the words 'White House' does not affect the reader other than to provide a warning that the moment has arrived to switch from the script on the prompter to the script on the desk. Occasional disasters occur at this point with inexperienced readers, but in the main these are avoided with practice.

Alterations, provided they are clear, can be written in by hand if necessary, while late additions or deletions of a substantial size are made to the prompter script by cutting across the roll with a pair of scissors, inserting the extra paper and joining the cut ends with sticky tape or a quick-drying glue. Either operation need take only a few seconds.

Where time is too short for changes to be made, the operator simply writes

> Read Page No. 15a

as an instruction for the reader to rely on his own script.

The latest generation of Autocue equipment avoids the need to re-type scripts, for it is able to handle the standard four-inch prompter roll *and* material on A4 or foolscap paper.

All in all, prompting devices have proved a real boon to news performers and have helped add such a cool, slick look to production that it is difficult to know how any modern television news programme can afford to be without them.

Interviewing

Probably more indignation is aroused by interviews than almost any other aspect of factual television, even though the objections arise less frequently over news interviews than over those which come under the loose heading of 'current affairs'.

Complaints tend to fall into three categories. First, there is the matter of intrusion, where instead of respecting the privacy of, say, the newly bereaved, interviewers are seen and heard callously asking questions apparently without a qualm. Any questioning in these circumstances would seem to be extremely difficult to justify in a civilised society, yet the fact remains that a surprising number of people are willing, even anxious, to talk about their tragic experiences, either as a form of mental release or as a genuine attempt to avoid similar occurrences happening to others.

Certainly some reporters are guilty of overstepping the mark by asking penetrating questions of those still too stunned to realise quite what they are saying. But such interviews have long been considered legitimate journalistic practice, and will no doubt remain so. The most that can be asked of television reporters is that they put their questions with tact and sympathy and do not demand answers as of right.

The second category of complaint concerns the attitude taken towards the subject being interviewed. There is no doubt that there is a substantial body of opinion which takes exception to *any* form of questioning that seems to probe beyond the straightforward elicitation of facts. This objection is usually framed as a question: 'How *dare* they?' or "What qualifies the interviewer to ask anything else?" Rather more serious are the criticisms levelled against those whose techniques smack of bullying, the ". . . very skilful (not to say ruthless) questioning by young men highly trained in 'loading and leading'".[1]

At its worst, this technique has been termed 'trial by television', and has been most graphically illustrated by programmes in which interviewees have been browbeaten into making some-

---

[1]Bishop George Clarkson, letter to *The Times*, April 7, 1975.

Speeding up the newsgathering process. Chartering an aircraft instead of waiting for a scheduled flight, particularly on busy or crowded routes, is a method often used to move camera crews quickly into position. Customs clearance procedures can be completed and equipment transferred to other transport in a very short time. (*Michael Sullivan*)

Page ii: Looking for a better shot. BBC Television News team hill-climbing in Sardinia in search of panoramic views to include in a news feature. Close cooperation between reporter and crew on location is essential. If maximum value is to be extracted from words *and* pictures the journalist must know in detail what is in the camera. That means being on the spot to make a note of every shot.

Page ii: Piece to camera. The right background is essential. It must always be relevant and interesting yet not divert the viewer's attention from the reporter's words. The sound recordist kneels out of the way of the camera so that he can use the rifle mike at close range.

(*R. M. K. Wheaton*)

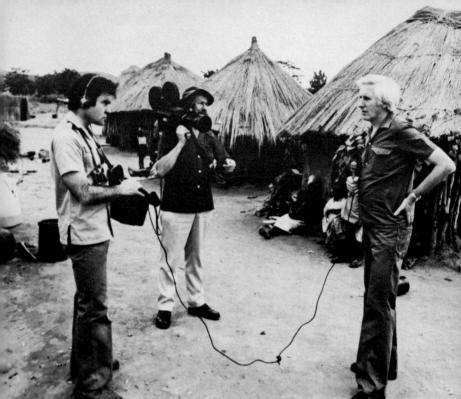

Dressing the part. BBC reporter Michael Sullivan in a safari suit for this report from an African village. Jacket and tie would have been uncomfortable and entirely out of place. (See Speech, mannerisms and dress, pp 96-98). *(BBC Central Stills)*

Silent and sound. Contrast of two cameramen at work in Belfast. One uses an easily-managed Bell & Howell mute camera with three-lens turret; the other has an Arriflex BL with zoom lens. Note the Swedish camera-man's chest harness to keep the camera steady. His recordist is out of picture, at the other end of the trailing cable.

(Michael Sullivan)

Page iv: The Newsreader's friend. An Autocue studio prompting device in action. The drive unit, left, incorporates a tiny television camera which scans the typed prompter roll or page of script; a mirror device superimposes the words on to the front of the camera, allowing the reader to look straight out at the viewer as he speaks.

(Autocue Products)

Page iv. Electronic newsgathering (ENG). The lightweight electronic camera system which is taking television news into a new era. Pictures can be recorded on to videotape cassette on location, transmitted 'live', or beamed to home base for recording and editing. The equipment is still undergoing development, but is already playing a growing role in newsgathering operations, particularly in the United States. *(BBC Central Stills)*

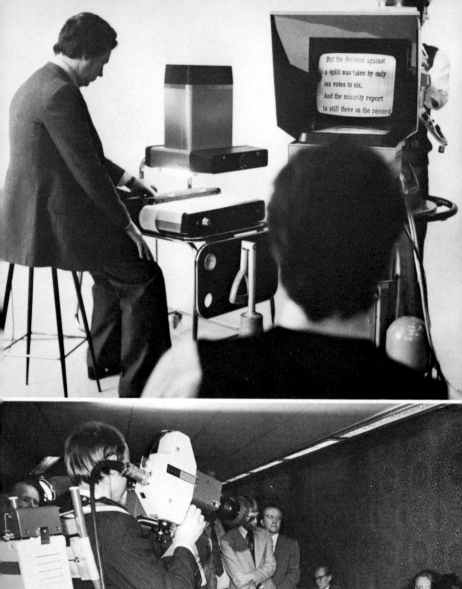

But the decision against
a split was taken by only
ten votes to six.
And the minority report
is still there on the record.

times damaging personal admissions by relentless questioning bordering on interrogation.

This entertainment is conducted on behalf of millions of viewers and, sometimes, a studio audience composed at least partly of those allegedly wronged by the subject of the interview. A secondary complaint is that the interviewers seem as much concerned with projecting their own already considerable egos as in producing serious answers to serious issues.

But perhaps it was only to be expected that the pendulum would swing so far the other way, after the bland, deferential questioning prevalent in the early fifties, when interviewers seemed entirely content with any platitudes uttered by public figures, shrinking back from querying the answers, however unenlightening.

The precise moment at which a recognisable change of attitude took place is impossible to identify, although many television news professionals consider the interview between Robin Day and President Nasser of Egypt in Cairo for ITN in 1957 to be a watershed. Here was a head of state answering with apparent frankness and sincerity questions which diplomats would probably have hesitated to ask. It was done politely, yet firmly, creating a real impact on the viewing audience and, unknown to the participants, setting a pattern for the future.

Since then attempts have been made to strike a reasonable balance between a persistent, unshakeable seeking after truth and the asking of legitimate questions in a non-truculent manner.

At the same time, many present-day interviewees have become just as conversant with the rules of the game as the interviewers, so they are well able to look after themselves in any verbal fisti-cuffs. Much of this has had to do with the television schools created by enterprising businessmen, often ex-television inter-viewers themselves, for the sole purpose of grooming would-be 'spokesmen' of all types for the battleground of the television studio or film interview. Some interviewers have raised objections on the grounds that such preparations are designed only to help equip the interviewee with enough skill to evade awkward questions. But these schools are here to stay, and it seems churlish for the professionals to quibble because the odds, always stacked against the interviewee, should have become slightly more even.

In any case, the able, intelligent, well-briefed interviewer should always be capable of extracting something worthwhile in the course of reasoned argument. Where there *is* evidence of evasion, the reporter should not hesitate to pursue, although without bullying. That is ill-mannered, unnecessary and certainly almost always counter-productive, since viewers are much more likely to be sympathetic towards anyone they regard as the underdog. Besides, an evasion or point-blank refusal to answer speaks eloquently enough for itself.

The third area of controversy concerns the editing of interviews. Politicians and other public figures who are frequently interviewed for television are by now well aware that in countries where editorial freedom exists not all that they have to say is going to find its way on to the screen, however important they consider it to be. Even where 'live' contributions are concerned, they know that there is never likely to be enough time available to rehearse all the arguments in the issue at hand, and are therefore content to try to restrict themselves to making the few main points essential to their platform, in the belief that even minimal exposure to the public is far better than none.

It is usually from the interviewee inexperienced in the ways of television that the loudest cries of 'misrepresentation' are invariably heard, and there can be only sympathy for those whose parenthetical remarks are construed as the real substance and are extracted for use from a recorded interview. In *all* cases reporters should make it clear that they are under no obligation to use the whole of an interview, or indeed any of it, and give the subject an opportunity to make out a case in a cogent fashion or withdraw altogether.

Neither should any doubts be left about intended usage: an interviewee has the right to be told of the context in which the contribution is being made, and whether contrary opinions are being sought from others on the same subject. For, although it would be intolerable for journalists to lose the freedom to edit as they think fit, they should be equally jealous in guarding the rights of their interviewees to fair and honest treatment.

Four main forms of news interview

Interviews represent probably the highest proportion of contributions made by television reporters to news programmes, even though they may be of miniscule duration and the credits given collectively ('We asked the general secretary . . .') rather than individually ('Tom Harrison asked the general secretary . . .').

Of all the different types seen on the screen, possibly the one presently in most frequent use is the *set-piece*, conducted on the

110

interviewee's own territory, in some other appropriate setting, or in the news studio itself for recorded or live transmission. (See pages 123–124). The important thing about the set-piece is that it presupposes the interviewee's willingness to participate, and that arrangements are usually made far enough in advance for the reporter to do some proper homework, including the preparation of questions.

Such luxuries are not normally afforded reporters assigned to *eye-witness* or *spot interviews*, where the most important journalistic quality in demand is the speedy rooting out of those willing and able to talk about their experiences of events which may just have occurred. The questions here are more likely to concern facts rather than opinions.

Much the same can be said of the *doorstepper*, which is probably the form of questioning most loathed by reporter and subject alike. The reporter waits, perhaps literally on the doorstep of a building (hence the name), in order to snatch a few words, any words, with the main participant in some newsworthy event.

These hit-and-miss affairs are scarcely worthy of the name 'interview', yet they have become familiar sights on many a nation's television screen. In the general melée all too often involved, the television reporter may get no further than thrusting the microphone forward to ask such basic questions as "What's been happening?" or "What's next?" in the hope that what may start out as non-committal, even grudging answers may, with patience, become proper interviews in which some real information is forthcoming. Even the refusal to say anything more than "no comment" is often considered worthwhile screening if only to show the manner of rebuff.

This random method of interviewing is one stage removed from the *vox pop* (*vox populi*), an entertaining but inconsequential sounding of opinion among people, usually ordinary members of the public, stopped in the street. The aim is to achieve a cross-section of views on a specific topic, with each contribution usually boiled down to one or two pithy comments lasting a few seconds. The technique demands that the same question be put in the same way each time so that the answers may be edited together without the interviewer popping up in between to spoil the flow.

All interviews may be said to be variations on these four broad themes, including the ubiquitous *news conference* so beloved of politicians. This is meant to obviate the need for separate interviews, so is usually held somewhere large enough to accommodate all the television, radio and press people who want to attend. On occasions the numbers run into hundreds, presenting enormous difficulties for the television news reporter, who may not even get the opportunity to put a single question.

At other times paths may be smoothed by the organisers' imposition of an advance order of questioning, but this can be taken to extremes, as those who attended the superbly stage-managed 'news conferences' conducted by President de Gaulle will testify.

Settings for news conferences, as for many other newsworthy happenings, take any choice of location for questioning entirely out of the hands of the reporter and film crew. Then it is a matter of making do with whatever site is available, relying on good picture composition and sound quality to make the result as satisfactory as possible.

Far more desirable from the reporter's point of view is the selection of a background appropriate to the particular story. It makes far more sense to interview the scientist in the laboratory rather than in front of a plain office wall, to talk to the newspaper editor against a background of bustling newsroom activity, to the shop floor worker on the shop floor, and so on. Relevance should always be the aim where possible.

One word of caution. There is a very fine line between a background of interest and one so absorbing that it distracts the viewer from what is being said. Being too clever can also create unexpected problems with editing. I once chose to locate an interview with the managing director of a motor firm on the brow of a hill overlooking the company's test track. It was certainly relevant, the cars making a very pleasant sight as they whizzed across from one side of the picture to the other behind the interviewee's back. Unfortunately, it dawned on us only in the cutting room afterwards that one particularly crucial editing point came at the precise moment that a car was in motion half way across the screen, and that a straight cut into a later section of the interview had the effect of making it vanish into thin air.

Although the composition of the picture is the responsibility of the cameraman, it is a poor reporter who allows the subject to be so badly framed that trees or other obstacles appear to be growing out of the interviewee's head. On one occasion a serious interview was reduced to near farce when it was discovered, too late, that what was apparently an ideal background of swords hung horizontally on the wall had wholly unexpected results when viewed

on the two-dimensional television screen: a long, heavy blade
appeared to protrude from the side of the subject's neck. And
what made it all the more fascinating was that he did not seem to
notice it.

Putting the questions

Most journalists have had considerable experience as interviewers before they come to television, but there is a vast difference
between the casual questioning which takes place in the quiet
corner of a pub or over the telephone and the paraphernalia of
lighting, camera equipment and perspiring technicians.

The newspaper journalist is able to phrase the questions in a
conversational, informal manner, interjecting now and again to
clarify a point, jotting down answers with pencil and notebook.
Questions and answers need not be grammatical or even follow a
logical pattern. The same ground may be gone over again and
again. If either protagonist has a cleft palate, hair lip or some
other impediment, no matter. The printed page on which the
interview appears does not communicate that fact to the reader,
without the writer deliberately choosing to do so. In television,
journalistic judgement and writing ability alone are not enough.

Sir Geoffrey Cox, one time editor of ITN saw the significant
difference between the two forms of interview very early on in the
history of British television news:

> "The best newspaperman will often take plenty of time
> stalking around his subject, taking up minor points before he
> comes to his main question, noting a fact here, or an emphasis
> there, and then sifting out his material later when he sits
> down at the typewriter. But the television journalist is forced
> to go to the point at once, as bluntly and curtly as is practic-
> able. His questions must also be designed to produce
> compact answers. In this sense he has to be sub-editing his
> final story as he goes along, for although film can be cut, it
> cannot be compressed."[1]

Michael Parkinson, an experienced practitioner in both newspaper and television interviewing, puts it more forcefully, summing up the newspaper interview as 'child's play', compared with
that for television.

[1] *The Daily Telegraph*, July 7, 1958.

"A three-hour chat over lunch, a carefully written, honed and edited piece and the journalist has created something that is generally beyond the reach of any interviewer on television who tries to do his job without the luxury of being able to shape his material after the event. One is instant journalism, the other retrospective. It is the difference between riding bareback and sitting astride a rocking horse."[1]

Not every television interviewer would put it as baldly as that, but it is undoubtedly true that the screen interview of any type, live, filmed or recorded on to videotape, makes considerably more demands on the person conducting it. The essential requirements include an ability to think quickly to follow up topics outside the originally planned structure of the interview, and a capacity to marshal the thoughts in a way which builds up logical, step-by-step answers. Each interview, however brief, is capable of taking on a recognisable shape. Questions which are sprayed in all directions as topics are chosen at random only make the live interview difficult to follow and the recorded one doubly hard to edit intelligently. In any case 'the office' would much prefer to select a chunk of two or three questions and answers which follow a logical progression.

Apart from that, there is the undoubted waste of money involved in the exposing of film on questions and answers which have no real relevance to the occasion and will inevitably end up on the cutting room floor. The same goes for any attempt to produce a relaxed atmosphere by lobbing one or two innocuous 'warm-up' questions at the beginning.

In addition, the actual phrasing of questions needs to be considered. Too many inexperienced reporters, rather fond of the sound of their own voices in the early stages of their careers, tend to make long, rambling statements barely recognisable as questions at all. At the other extreme are the brusque, two or three word interjections which, apart from anything else, do not register on the screen long enough if faithfully repeated as cutaways (see page 122). Next come the clichés, of which these are my favourite examples:

How/What do you feel (about) . . . ?
Just what/how much/how serious . . . ?
What of the future . . . ?

---

[1] *The Sunday Times*, December 15, 1974.

Then there is the tendency to preface virtually every question with some deferential phrase or other which is presumably meant to soften up the interviewee:

May I ask . . . ?
Do you mind my asking . . . ?
What would you say if I asked . . . ?
Could you tell me . . . ?
Might I put it like this . . . ?

each of which invites curt rejection. Shooting straight from the hip has its drawbacks, of course. Without proper care, questions which are *too* direct are quite likely to produce a simple "yes" or "no", without further elaboration:

Is it true you've resigned because of a personal disagreement with the Prime Minister?

Is there any chance that you might return to the government?

Have you decided what you're going to do next?

If the television news interview is to be of any worth at all, the questions must be constructed more skilfully, in ways designed to draw out positive replies:

What do you say about reports that you've resigned because of a personal disagreement with the Prime Minister?

How would things have to change before you'd consider returning to the government?

What are you planning to do next?

As for general demeanour, every interviewer should be polite yet firm in pursuit of answers to legitimate questions, refusing to be overawed in the presence of the important or powerful, or overbearing when the subject of the interview is unused to television. As Robin Day once put it in a ten-point code he suggested as far back as 1961:

". . . a television interviewer is not employed as a debater, prosecutor, inquisitor, psychiatrist or third-degree expert, but as a journalist seeking information on behalf of the viewer."[1]

---

[1] *Television: A Personal Report* (Hutchinson, 1961).

Sometimes, in seeking that information from an agreeable and fluent interviewee, it is tempting to try out the questions in a 'dry run' without the camera. That is a mistake. First of all, no journalist worth his salt ever compromises himself or his employers by submitting questions in advance. Secondly, any interview based on known questions is almost certain to lack any feeling of spontaneity. Thirdly, even the most apparently loquacious people are inclined to 'talk themselves out' during a formal try-out, becoming tongue-tied when the real thing begins. So while a brief discussion about the general scope of an interview is a sensible preliminary, any full-scale rehearsal should be eschewed.

Coping with the answers

It is all very well for the reporter to ask the questions the average member of the public would dearly love the opportunity to put. Actually coping with the answers poses a problem by itself.

The experienced politician is quite capable of turning aside the most difficult question with a disarming smile and a reference to the interviewer by Christian name. Others are just as adept at totally ignoring the meaning of any question and ploughing on regardless with an entirely different and prepared answer. In either case the reporter's response ought to be a dogged repetition, hoping that the viewer will spot any evasion.

The reporter's real troubles begin, however, when he does not listen to the answers. That is by no means as uncommon as it might seem. The pressure on a questioner conducting a film interview can be almost as great as on the interviewee and it is all too easy to concentrate on mentally ticking off a list of prepared questions instead of listening, poised to follow up with an occasional supplementary. If the reporter lets this happen any number of obvious loose ends may remain untied. Ideally, it should be possible to forget the camera and the rest of it, relying on sound journalistic instinct to take over.

Some other small points: jumping in too soon with a new question before the interviewee has finished the old one produces an ugly overlap of two voices, and is also uneditable. If an interruption is necessary, wait until the subject pauses for breath. If the question is genuinely misunderstood, the reply halting, gobbledy-gook or totally off course in some other way, the reporter is well advised to call out 'cut' to stop the camera so that the problem can be discussed before restarting the interview. This is far preferable

116

to stumbling through until the bitter end and then deciding to try all over again.

Filmed interview, step by step
  As an example of the way a typical set-piece news interview might be conducted, consider the steps taken in this fictionalised question and answer session in the third floor office of an economics adviser. Assume that both participants have been adequately briefed. Time is important as the reporter has an early-evening programme deadline to meet and the adviser has to leave for an important meeting within half an hour.

  Step one, setting up: The office is of medium size, the furniture consisting of a large desk with a swivel chair behind it, one easy chair and a coat stand. The only natural light comes from a single window overlooking the main road and heavy traffic. The team's equipment, having been manhandled from the lift a few yards away, now litters the floor. The sound recordist unstraps the legs on the tripod which the cameraman then sets up opposite but slightly left of the interviewee's chair some twelve feet away. The camera is mounted firmly on to the tripod head, the cameraman consulting the built-in spirit level to make sure that the picture will be absolutely straight as well as steady. A straight-backed chair for the reporter is brought in from an outer office and placed about three feet to the left of the camera, at about seven o'clock (Fig. 28). Meanwhile the lighting assistant, having found the office power outlet socket, is asked by the cameraman to put up three 800 W lights. All are extended to their full height so that the lamps can be angled towards the swivel chair without blinding the person who is to sit in it. One becomes the 'key' light behind the reporter's chair, the second is placed to the right of the camera to fill in the shadows, and the third behind the subject to provide backlight. This, then is the classic interview set-up, with the camera in position as the observer of a discussion between two people. But as it will concentrate entirely on the interviewee, compensation has to be made for any impression that no one else is involved. For this reason the lens looks over the reporter's shoulder, framing the subject in three-quarter full face, slightly off-centre and looking across the empty side of the screen towards the questioner (Figs. 29a and 29b). Moving the camera further to the left would have the interviewee looking directly into the lens (Fig. 30a), suggesting a party political broadcast or some form of appeal. More to the right would produce a full profile, making him look right out of the picture—television's equivalent of allowing the subject of an end-column newspaper photograph to face out of the page (Fig. 30b). The height of the camera is set so that the cameraman's view is two or three inches above the subject's line of sight (eyeline, Fig. 31). Going below the eyeline and looking up has a distorting effect.

Step two, final preparations: The two main characters emerge from an outer office, where they have been having a brief talk about the area the interview is intended to cover, although the reporter has been careful not to divulge the detailed questions. All three lights are switched on, the venetian blind on the window firmly closed against traffic noise and to prevent an awkward mix of artificial and daylight. With his exposure meter, the cameraman approaches the interviewee and carefully measures the light falling on head and shoulders. From the reading he sets the aperture on the camera. The recordist has already settled on light, individual microphones as the most suitable for the occasion (see page 142). He hands one to the reporter, then goes to the opposite side of the desk fastening the other loosely round the neck of the interviewee, under his tie, slipping the lead under his jacket out of sight of the lens. Now, with the amplifier cable plugged into the sound output socket at the back of the camera, the recordist asks each participant in the interview for a quick burst of 'level' to ensure that both voices are heard with equal volume. Traffic noise from the street three floors below is minimal, thanks to the window blind, but the sound of the typewriter intrudes through the thin office wall and the recordist asks the secretary next door to stop for a few minutes and also to prevent any telephone calls from interrupting. Satisfied, he squats on the camera box a few feet from the camera, making sure not to trip over the amplifier lead. The lighting assistant stands by one of the lights in front of the desk, careful not to throw a shadow; the reporter refers again to the questions scribbled on his notepad and switches on the tiny cassette tape recorder he has also

Fig. 28. Classic interview position. Camera looks over interviewer's shoulder. Subject is framed in three-quarter full face, looking towards questioner, not into camera lens.

Fig. 29. (a) Framing here is too square.

Fig. 29. (b) Subject should be set slightly to one side, looking across the empty side of frame.

Fig. 30. (a) Too square suggests 'party political' or other appeal.

Fig. 30. (b) 'Profile' shot has subject looking too far out of frame.

Fig. 31. Camera height set to give cameraman a view of two or three inches above subject's eyeline.

brought along. The cameraman plugs in the battery to drive the camera motor, makes one final exposure reading as a precaution and gives the focus on the 10:1 zoom lens a fine adjustment.

Step three, interview in progress: "Quiet please," calls the cameraman. A second or so later, he flicks the motor switch forward on to the 'on' position and looks for the pulsating red light at the back of the camera which indicates that the film is beginning to roll from the full 400 ft magazine loaded at the end of the previous assignment. For the first six or seven seconds he films what is known as a silent establishing two-shot, taking in the back of the reporter's head, the interviewee and the top of the desk, to show the physical relationship between those taking part. As long as the interviewee has been warned not to speak at this stage, the two-shot can be dropped in by the film editor over any of the questions or used as a means of condensing the discussion if necessary. This shot complete, the cameraman now frames the interviewee on his own, calling out 'action,' 'running' or simply 'go ahead' as a cue for the reporter to begin asking the questions. As a typical news interview is rarely longer than six questions, the cameraman goes through his usual sequence of shots using the zoom lens to give a pleasing visual variation and aid swift editing later. He does this without stopping the camera or the interview but makes sure any movement is made only during the questions, and not the answers, which would make editing more difficult. He holds the first few questions and answers in a steady medium shot, from the waist up (Fig. 32a). As the third question is being asked he tightens to a medium close-up, from the chest upwards (Fig. 32b); during the fifth he focuses in still further to a close-up of the head and shoulders (Fig. 32c). Exposed at twenty five frames per second (fps), 16 mm film goes through the camera at a rate of one hundred feet every two minutes and forty seconds, so nearly two hundred and fifty feet have been used by the time the last question has been answered after six and three quarter minutes. At that point the reporter calls out firmly "cut". The cameraman switches off, asks the lighting assistant to turn out ('kill') the three lights, which have made the room rather warm, and inquires whether that is all. Yes thanks, says the reporter.

Fig. 32. (a) Medium shot (from the waist up).

Fig. 32. (b) Medium close up (from the chest up).

Fig. 32. (c) Close up (head and shoulders).

Fig. 33. (a) Cameraman's rule for cut-away questions. The ear the camera sees during the interview . . .

Fig. 33. (b) . . . is the same one the cameraman must see in the cut-away, wherever the interviewer is positioned.

The interviewee is helped out of the microphone round his neck, excuses himself and departs for his meeting about fifteen minutes earlier than he expected.

Step four, cutaway questions: Now comes the time to complete the *cutaways* (*cut-ins* or *reverses*). These are the questions, repeated by the reporter on film for possible use by the film editor in bridging different sections of the interview. The reporter plays back the conversation as recorded on his tape cassette, noting both the phrasing of each question and the tone of voice. He jots them down alongside the original notes he made as a guideline. The cameraman now intends to concentrate on the face of the reporter, which he was unable to do during the course of the interview. It means moving either the reporter or the camera to a new position. The cameraman concludes that in this case it is simplest to ask the reporter to move his chair round, and to adjust the lighting set-up accordingly. Now he re-focuses, taking great pains to ensure that the reporter's eyeline is correct. If it is not, the edited film would give the impression that the interviewer and subject were looking in the same direction instead of at each other. To make sure there is no slip, the cameraman follows the simple rule he made for himself years before: the ear that the camera saw during the interview proper must be the same ear the camera sees in the cutaway questions (Fig. 33a and 33b). As a further refinement, the interviewer is filmed in a medium shot, so that whatever portion is chosen from the film the reporter will seem to complement rather than dominate the subject. The questions themselves follow the original sequence. Although they are now being asked of no one, the reporter tries hard to re-create the spontaneity of the interview several minutes earlier, taking the opportunity to tidy up one or two small grammatical errors. After each of the cutaways, he looks down at his pad to refresh his memory, making a deliberate pause of two or three seconds before asking the next. He knows that if he speaks while still looking down at his notes the film editor will find that question impossible to use.

To finish, the reporter may do several 'noddies', fairly vigorous nods of the head to simulate reactions as they might have occurred at various points during the interview. They serve the same purpose as cutaway questions, acting as bridges between edited sections. But reporters, in general, seem unable to carry them out with much conviction and the technique has begun to fall into disuse. There is also a growing, uncomfortable awareness among newspeople that in some interviews 'noddies' might create the wrong impression for the audience, misleading them into believing that the reporter agreed with what was said.

As an alternative, cameramen film 'steady listening shots' of an attentive but otherwise immobile reporter and, where time allows, a close-up listening shot of the *subject* is also added to give the film editor a maximum choice of cutaway material.

Studio interviewing

Interviewing in a television studio or at the site of an outside broadcast is, in many ways, far less complicated than interviewing on film, despite the necessary presence of additional technical staff and equipment.

To broadcast a typical interview between two people, most studio directors employ at least two electronic cameras, one to concentrate largely on the reporter. Separate cutaways at the end should therefore be unnecessary, making editing of interviews linked to videotape fast and relatively simple.

As parts of news programmes rather than as programmes in their own right, live interviews have the undoubted merit of being malleable. Those which are not getting anywhere can be savagely shortened. Really good ones can be allowed to continue at the expense of other items dropped during transmission. Then there are some producers who will happily tailor their interviews to fit whatever odd spaces remain in their programmes without much regard to quality. More still have had cause to be thankful for the interviews which were able to fill a void created by a sudden breakdown of videotape or telecine.

The satisfaction for those conducting any one of these battles of wit is that the outcome depends on the judgement and ability of the reporter alone, and has to stand without the benefit of editing after the event. The techniques required are generally no different from those used in other types of interview, except that the reporter probably needs to be more mentally alert than ever, and that deeper briefing is needed to ensure there is no 'drying up'.

The one extra skill which has to be developed is a sense of timing. The interview must not be so hurried that there is nothing left to say and time still to spare. Neither must there be such dalliance over the first part that important ground remains to be covered and the interviewee has to be cut off in full flight.

Helping to achieve that fine degree of timing is the floor manager, an important member of the production staff, who is positioned out of camera range yet within clear signalling sight of the interviewer.

Various timings are given as the interview proceeds, the most crucial period being the final minute. A circular 'winding up' motion of the hand indicates the last thirty seconds, time enough for the interview to be brought to a smooth conclusion. The final 10 seconds are counted down separately, by finger signal. At zero, the floor manager executes a cut-throat sign to show that time has run out. The most experienced interviewers have become really adept at this timing exercise, able to wring the very last ounce of value from their interviews right up to the dying seconds.

PACKAGING THE NEWS

ON numerous occasions, a brief interview or a simple piece to camera is all that a reporter will be asked to contribute to a news programme. That each calls for its own special kind of expertise should now be in doubt. Yet an infinitely greater test of a reporter's television technique comes when those hard-won individual skills have to be welded together in the form of a news *package*, a film or videotaped report which appears on the screen complete in itself apart from the news 'peg' read by the newsreader in the studio.

The construction of any successful package requires more than the performing talents so apparent in the piece to camera, or the stubborn persistence needed in some interviews. It demands conscious organisation, the facility to fit different pieces together to produce an effective continuous narrative, and a newswriter-like mastery over words and pictures. And when all that is accomplished, the accompanying documentation must be so thorough that the report is capable of being assembled quickly and accurately by other people, no matter how far away.

Not that packages have to be complicated just because they are invariably of substantial duration. Experienced reporters and crews, working closely towards a common goal, are well aware of the dangers of wild over-shooting, while at the same time making quite sure that they do not skimp their coverage in any way.

Broken down into its separate components, a typical package might appear to the viewer in the following order:

1. Picture sequence accompanied by the reporter's out-of-vision commentary.
2. An interview.
3. More pictures and commentary, linking into.
4. A final piece to camera.

Yet the chances are that the sequence in which they were completed was very different.

Some news services like to stamp their own individual styles on film package formats, although these preferences may be only as straightforward as insisting they always begin with the reporter's piece to camera (to establish presence and authority at once) or never ending with an interview, expecting the reporter himself to complete the report with a visual pay-off.

But these are really minor considerations. From the reporter's point of view, the versatility of the package technique ranks high among its most satisfying aspects, with the separate ingredients capable of being mixed together in almost limitless quantity and sequence according to story demands. The one proviso is that during shooting reporter and cameraman keep the eventual shape firmly in mind, otherwise there is a strong likelihood that there will be too much or too little material to cover a particular section. The latter fault may make it impossible for the film editor to assemble the report without blatant disregard for accepted film grammar or else become involved in the difficult, time-consuming, reporter reputation-wrecking operation disparagingly known as 'a salvage job'.

Filmed report: an example

For an example of the way a typical film report might be constructed, take this routine, fictional piece about the increasing economic pressures on small dairy farmers. Assume the film has been commissioned by the programme editor to accompany an announcement of a rise in milk prices expected later the same day. Arrangements will have been made well in advance to secure the co-operation of the farm owner.

Although an unrepentant 'townie', the reporter has briefed himself sufficiently well on the subject of farming to be aware of the general ground the assignment is meant to cover. A short talk with the farmer immediately on arrival fills in the other necessary detail. The camera crew, meanwhile, take the opportunity to spy out the land without the encumbrance of their equipment, and the cameraman is already taken with the potential for vivid pictures.

Friendly, helpful and articulate, the farmer has a number of important duties to perform about the place and is anxious to complete his own part in the proceedings as quickly as possible.

126

The first ingredient, therefore, must be the interview which the reporter and cameraman originally envisaged taking place later on, set up against a background of the prize herd being milked. But the farmer's declared intentions have now forced a change of plan so, too early for the milking, they settle for an exterior view of the shed, with half a dozen milk churns clearly visible.

Six questions and answers follow smoothly, rounded off by the obligatory establishing two-shot and cutaway questions. Total so far, 200 ft.

The reporter and crew, left to themselves, decide after a brief discussion to concentrate on other buildings, activity, people and animals around the farm, working in from the perimeter towards the farmhouse, of which the cameraman shoots several feet of exteriors from different angles. Next they move inside to film the farmer's wife, who keeps the accounts, making her books up to date in the kitchen. All that takes another 150 ft.

Over a break for coffee the reporter, now able to anticipate how the rest of the filming will go, writes and memorises the script for a piece to camera, a little over 30 sec. summing up the dilemma for farmers of this type. Back outside, he asks to be framed in a fairly loose medium shot against a haystack background to emphasise a point about increased feeding costs. He is virtually at the end of the piece when an unseen tractor starts up noisily, drowning his voice. A second take is necessary, for which there is just enough film left on the 400 ft roll.

Before a new magazine can be fitted, milking time has suddenly arrived. In fact, the herd can be seen in the distance, already beginning to make their way up from the lower grazing field. The cameraman grabs his spare camera loaded with one hundred feet of silent film, stuffs two extra rolls into his jacket pocket, and makes off at a brisk trot with the reporter in pursuit. The cameraman is only just in time to get the shots he has been thinking about. Within a very few minutes he has exposed more than seventy feet of film on close and medium shots of the cows and cowmen on the move. He then runs to a conveniently elevated vantage point to film them in a long shot, holding it steady until the procession has passed in front of him out of the picture on its way to the milking shed.

Pausing only to load a new roll, he starts to follow at a leisurely pace. Then he sees the farmer emerge from an outhouse and engage one of the farmhands in animated conversation. On this scene he exposes about twenty feet before the farmer makes off in another direction and the cameraman stands his ground, following his progress through the camera viewfinder.

At the shed, milking is in progress. The sound recordist has already set up the sound camera on its tripod. positioning it close to where the action is taking place. The clatter of the machinery and the occasional lowing of the cows make effective sounds to accompany the pictures. After fifty feet, the cameraman is satisfied. Only one more shot, of the farm entrance, remains to be filmed, and that will be done on departure.

They begin to wrap up. The cameraman sorts through the equipment for packing away into the car. The recordist takes his tape machine out into the field to capture some 'wild' atmosphere sound to go with the material shot on the silent camera.

The reporter has found a quiet spot away from all the activity and has begun to replay his own cassette recording of the interview with the farmer. After hearing it once all the way through, he decides that the second and third answers are easily the most relevant, summing up the issues most succinctly. Timed on the stop-watch they account for a total of one minute and twenty five seconds. Too long, he considers, for a package he was told would be allocated no more than three minutes on the screen. Listening even more carefully he decides that by coming in later on the first of the chosen answers the interview can be pared down still further without destroying the core of the farmer's argument, although one particularly colourful reference to government policies is lost. Fifty seconds now. Much better. Going back over the rest of the interview again he makes notes about some of the other points raised, adding them to the references made during his original research. These are for possible use in the commentary he must now write to cover the rest of the film.

He was at pains to accompany the cameraman throughout the entire filming, and now he consults the list of shots he made clearly and in detail as they went along. With the full knowledge of the content and duration of each, he can visualise how the script will eventually sound and look on the screen. Without that essential information it would have been guesswork, and would have shown as such.

The rough outline of the package is beginning to fill in as the reporter starts to weave the commentary round the pictures. Conscious of the need to identify the location as quickly as possible, he opens by setting the scene, visualising the shots of the farm entrance yet to be taken:

As farms go, Topfield is very much in the miniature class, not even one hundred acres.

Next he wants to sketch in the background, as briefly as possible, in the context of the type of work being carried out. There were plenty of good shots of general activity on roll one, and he rejects the phrase 'pig-rearing' as being too explicit, favouring instead the all-purpose 'stock-breeding' so that the film editor will be able to choose the most suitable pictures:

> But, thanks to a mixture of stock-breeding and milk production, every one of the past twenty years has produced a profit. Until this year, that is, when despite increased production and higher government subsidies, Topfield—like so many farms of similar size—is facing a loss. It's potentially so crippling that the rise in the price of milk may be too late to save . . .

At this point, the commentary begins to approach the central issue of the prize Jerseys and their future. The reporter remembers the variation of shots taken by the cameraman as they were being moved from the lower grazing field, and he sees the sequence extending naturally to the noisy scenes in the milking shed. Although continuity must be maintained, he deliberately avoids too rigid a construction which would leave the film editor no scope to put in extra shots without having to make drastic alterations to the sound track:

> . . . the herd of seventy prize Jerseys from being sold off. Since the first of the cows was bought five years ago, the farm's annual average milk production has more than doubled. Recent investment in a new, automated milking system seemed certain to increase yields still further. Despite modernisation, things have gone seriously wrong.

The next paragraph leads to the interview with the farmer. For this, the reporter expects that the film editor will want to use the two-shot, taken with the milk churns in full view. The last few words have to pose the question, phrasing it in a way which makes the chosen answer follow naturally:

> Topfield's owner, Mr John Brown, has survived other years of crisis. What's different about this one?

Including the fifty seconds allocated to the interview the

reporter estimates that, depending on the way the milking sequence is eventually cut, between one minute forty five seconds and two minutes have so far been accounted for. That leaves a maximum of one minute fifteen seconds for the remaining ingredients, including the piece to camera, which took thirty two seconds. He makes the most of the obvious link between the farmer and the pictures of his wife and thinks the farmhouse exteriors make a neater transition than by going straight to Mrs Brown from the interview:

> The Browns bought Topfield when they married soon after the Second World War. At the time it was virtually run down, but Mrs Marjorie Brown, who used to spend weekends here helping out the previous owner, persuaded her husband it had potential.

If necessary, the reporter reckons, the next line could be omitted to save space, although it would be a pity:

> She comes from a farming family and had her own ideas about how to put matters right financially.

The final two sentences are important, about the future. Here the reporter is in two minds whether they are better illustrated by shots of the farmhands and general activity left over from the first sound roll, or the conversation between farmer and helper filmed on the silent camera. He decides to let the office choose:

> Now the Browns are considering that if the herd has to go, they might as well sell up completely. If they're hesitating, it's because they're in no doubts about what it would mean for their small workforce—redundancy, in an area where unemployment is already high.

The commentary leading on from the interview adds up to thirty five seconds. Adding on the piece to camera brings the total length to a maximum of three minutes and seven seconds. Just right, thinks the reporter. Six seconds can be saved by taking out the additional reference to the farmer's wife, a few more by keeping a tight hold on the prize herd sequence.

The whole scripting exercise has taken no more than twenty five minutes. Seeking out the recordist, now returned to the camera car, the reporter finds a place on the farm where no single sound is dominant, and records the commentary on to $\frac{1}{4}$in tape. He stumbles once, over the phrase "here helping out . . ." and after a deliberate pause substitutes "working here for . . ." for the offending words when he repeats the whole paragraph.

Later, in assembling the package, the film editor will depart from the usual procedure of cutting the film and letting the news-writer fit the commentary round it. This time, having re-recorded the $\frac{1}{4}$ in tape 'wild track' commentary on to 16mm sound track, the editor will be guided by the written script, laying the pictures over the matching words. This technique, known as *overlay*, has given modern television news reporting much of its professional gloss. In both construction and editing it is testing and fairly slow, but the best exponents of the art are capable of producing excel-lent results by following the cardinal rules of knowing in detail what the film material contains and writing to it. They are always prepared to adjust the commentary to make use of interesting picture sequences for which allowance might not have been originally made, and avoid over-scripting sections for which there are scarcely sufficient shots. Otherwise the film editor has no alternative but to cut back the commentary track. On this occasion, however, the reporter has done a tidy job.

With the commentary now recorded, the film crew take their leave of the farmer, the cameraman remembering to stop briefly for his final shots on the sound camera as they drive out of the farm gates. The whole operation has taken a little over three hours for a total of six hundred and ten feet of film. They now make for the nearby railway station, where they despatch the film by train before moving on to a new assignment a hundred miles to the north.

On the way, with the recordist driving, the cameraman labels the exposed tins of film and begins to write out the *dopesheet*, which details the content for the film editor. (See page 134.) There are carbon copies for the editorial and processing departments.

As planned, they arrive at the station with a clear half hour to spare before the next train. The reporter hauls his portable typewriter out of the car boot and goes to the waiting room, where he makes a rapid copy of the original scribbled script, adding film editing instructions in the margin. The result is shown overleaf. This is a typical example of a script with alternatives and information for film editing.

Milk Prices, Topfield Farm, January 14.   Harrison script.

Long shots entrance____/As farms go, Topfield is very much in the
Roll 4   miniature class -- not even a hundred acres.
                         But thanks to a

Exterior GVs farm_____/mixture of stockbreeding and milk production,
Roll 1   every one of the past twenty years has
                         resulted in a profit. Until this year, that
                         is, when despite increased production and
                         higher Govt. subsidies, Topfield -- like so
                         many farms of a similar size -- is facing a
                         loss. It's so crippling that the rise in the
Herd moving_____price of milk may be too late to save/the herd
Roll 2   of seventy prize Jerseys from being sold off.
                         Since the first of the cows were bought 5 yrs
                         ago, the farm's annual average milk
                         production has more than doubled.

Automatic milking_____/Recent investment in a new, automated milking
Roll 4   system seemed certain to increase yields
                         still further. Despite modernisation things
                         have gone seriously wrong.

2-shot_____/Topfield's owner, Mr John Brown, has survived
Roll 4   other years of crisis. What's different
                         about this one?

Interview, Roll 1.
Use 2nd answer beginning: "This time, we've not been able"
to end 3rd answer: "whatever the Government says." (50 sec. approx)

GVs farmhouse_____/The Browns bought Topfield when they married,
Exteriors   soon after the 2nd World War. At the time it
Roll 1   was virtually run down, but

Mrs B. kitchen_____/Mrs Marjorie Brown, who used to spend weekends
Roll 1   working here for the previous owner,
                         persuaded her husband it had potential. She
                        ⎧comes from a farming family and has her own
         (droppable)   ⎨ideas about how to put matters right
                        ⎩financially.

Farmer & cowman_____/Now the Browns are considering that if the
Roll 3   herd has to go they might as well sell up
                         completely.
                         If they're hesitating it's because they're
            (or)   in no doubts what that would mean for their
People working_____/small workforce -- redundancy, in an area
Roll 1   where unemployment is already high.

Take in Piece to Cam.
Roll 1 (Use 2nd take) Approx. 30 sec.

Script, dopesheet and film are put into an 'onion' bag, clearly marked with its destination, and deposited with the parcel department ready for the next train. A telephone call to the office is made to confirm that the assignment has been completed and the film will soon be speeding on its way. At the other end, the intake department makes arrangements for the precious bag to be picked up from the station as soon as the train arrives.

Indisputably, proper documentation takes time, and it is certainly not so valuable that it is worth missing the only available train or plane in order to get it done. Sometimes, any rough notes made during filming may have to suffice, or the full information given later by telephone or telex once 'the dust has settled'.

Nevertheless, the principle remains. Without explicit directions to go by, the film editor is forced to waste precious time going backwards and forwards through perhaps a very large footage, just to identify people, places and events of which he probably has very little foreknowledge. I have seen some really excellent material discarded in anger and frustration because, in the limited editing time available, there was no way in which anyone at the output end could see how it fitted into the overall pattern.

The cameraman's dopesheet, however sketchy, usually offers some help, but few cameramen take enough care over the identification of each roll of film as it is exposed. Most hold up the relevant number of fingers in front of the lens as a brief guide each time. But on too many occasions that is not sufficient. In all but the direst circumstances it does not seem to be asking too much for the crew to film a two or three second shot of a number written legibly on a piece of paper or, as a last resort, on the palm of the hand. Where sync sound is being used the roll number should not be necessary as long as each take is marked on the clapperboard and identified on the dopesheet.

On the occasion of our fictitious 'Topfield Farm' story, the film editor's task has been made lighter anyway because of the relatively small footage, although the cutter and the newswriter concerned are not impressed by the milking scenes which, shot without the benefit of any artificial lighting, are slightly under-exposed. They decide to drop that sequence, excising the reference to the 'new, automated milking system', but keeping the next sentence—"Despite modernisation, things have gone seriously wrong"—which stands quite happily in its own right, covered by a three-second extension of the moving herd pictures. To compensate fully for the lost milking scenes, they retain the 'optional'

Assignment	TOPFIELD FARM	(5 o'clock Report)

Date	Location		Laboratory	
Jan. 14	Topfield area		London	№ 6050

Camera Jones		Sound Smith		Stock	Mag	Mute
Mute ✓	Tape ✓	Combined ✓		Used	480 ft.	130 ft.
Film Type		Ring if forced		Waste	20 ft.	∕
16mm 7240		1 2 3		Balance	∕	∕

Roll 1 Commag (400 ft)
Interview Farmer JOHN BROWN
2-shot + TOM HARRISON cutaway questions
Various shots piggery, chickens, farm activity,
people working
Exteriors farmhouse, interiors kitchen
+ MRS MARJORIE BROWN
Harrison piece to camera (Use 2nd take)

Roll 2 Mute (400ft.)
Prize cows being moved for milking
(Various shots)

Roll 3 Mute (30ft.)
Farmer Brown + Farmhand talking

Roll 4 Commag (80ft.)
Interiors milking shed
Exteriors farm entrance

+ 1 Roll ¼" tape general farm activity
+ HARRISON wild-track

Note — Script Enclosed

reference to Mrs Brown. The pictures in her kitchen, shot by the light streaming in through a modern patio window, have real quality.

Unaware of the circumstances, however, the two of them curse the cameraman roundly for not using the sound camera to shoot the farmer's brief conversation with one of his farmhands, but as the reporter's commentary covers most of it they decide this scene is preferable to the additional farm activity shots, which they find somewhat repetitive. Otherwise, it has been an efficiently-conducted operation all round, and with two other news stories unexpectedly yielding very little, the programme editor is more than content to take the report at its full length of two minutes and fifty five seconds—almost exactly the duration the reporter had calculated.

Getting the story, paperwork and duration right is not the extent of the reporter's responsibility. Just as much effort is needed to ensure that even before it reaches the transmission stage the package is not outdated, either by a commentary which makes no allowance for the time-gap between the collection of the material and its screening, or by ignoring any possibility that other events might affect its significance.

In the example of Topfield Farm, the reporter's script has deliberately made no more than a passing reference to the expected milk price rise, on the basis of which the report was originally commissioned. The phrase ". . . and the rise in the price of milk may be too late . . ." remains relevant no matter what size the increase or its date of implementation.

In addition, the sensible assumption has been made that the full details will have been given in the studio introduction written by the newswriter from other sources, and read by the newsreader as the lead-in to the film:

> Milk is going up in price. The rise, one penny a pint, takes effect from midnight. The government says it's necessary because the cost of fertiliser for cattle feed is making it uneconomical for some dairy farmers to carry on producing milk. Union leaders and consumer protection groups have already criticised the rise as sure to increase the burden on poorer families. The farmers themselves say one penny extra isn't nearly enough to prevent some going out of business. Tom Harrison has been finding out what difference a price increase would make for one farmer.

How the 'hard' facts of a news story are normally shared between studio newsreader and reporter is a matter for item-by-item assessment. Without formal apportionment, which is impractical, the prime objective is to ensure at almost any cost that the reporter's script, particularly at the beginning, does something more positive than repeat word for word what the newsreader has only just finished saying.

Although the temptation to take in *all* the major details is at times practically overwhelming, the reporter has an inescapable obligation to the newsroom to leave at least some of them for the introduction, however much of a sacrifice that may appear to be. Otherwise, the choice of alternatives left open to those at the output end may rest between the evils of a bland, uninformative introduction (which no news programme editor would tolerate) and surgery, the carving out of some of the facts from the report itself for use as part of the introduction.

Fortunately, the need for such drastic action is usually unnecessary. After a sharp lesson or two most reporters soon learn an acceptable level of self-discipline. Some achieve it by writing a full introduction of perhaps three sentences, each completely self-contained, and beginning the commentary proper with the *third*. The other two sentences are then sent off with the script details to provide introductory information for the newswriter. This admirably simple technique is capable of being practised by any reporter any time anywhere. Yet it still manages to create problems for those whose imaginations are not all that they might be. Deprived of the two most obvious opening sentences, some reporters are reduced to beginning the third in a form which, instead of helping the viewer to pick up the thread formed by the introduction, has become a cliché—a back reference to the event as

"It/The explosion/collision/accident . . . happened."

Mute and tape

The sophisticated overlay package, undoubtedly popular though it may have become, is far from being the only method currently used to produce comprehensive news film reports. Even though execution in the field need not necessarily take long to accomplish, as we have seen the technique makes considerable demands on film-editing time and expertise. It is also expensive simply in money terms. Not all news organisations can run to sufficient numbers of sound units to cover every assignment each day, no matter how routine.

Most, however, do have on tap the services of 'mute' men. These are single-person units equipped with hand-held, silent cameras, and a well-proven technique. They are employed to the best advantage using accompanying sound from a separate tape recorder. Pictorial subjects, particularly, lend themselves to this *mute and tape* treatment. The tape is used on location to record effects, with the reporter adding commentary later, or vice versa, although despite the efficiency of modern dubbing technique, the accurate reproduction of a whole range of very specific sounds throughout an entire film presents almost insuperable problems.[1] Where the luxury of a sound mixing facility exists at base, both effects and commentary can be recorded consecutively on the spot. In either case, film editing techniques remain the same as for the full-scale package, with the sound tracks re-recorded on sepmag. For the less well-off, the $\frac{1}{4}$ in tape itself can be cut to fit the pictures and the sound reproduced independently, in parallel, on transmission.

Double-chaining is another form of overlay. Instead of transferring the sound to sepmag, the film editor cuts two separate films, one with a commag track, the other with mute overlay material. On transmission the two films are run simultaneously, the director punching in the sound from the commag roll to cover the overlay.

Overlay in camera

A halfway stage between mute and tape and the sophisticated package is *overlay in camera*. This employs a sound crew and a simplified overlay technique to keep editing to a minimum and ensure the economical use of film.

Here, the report is constructed in its correct sequence. Thorough planning and some rehearsal are essential to ensure that cameraman and reporter keep exactly in step, as the commentary is

---

[1]Dubbing a commentary, if time permits, is an admirable alternative to using the overlay system, for it is added only after the pictures have been edited. The film is shown on a large screen while the words are recorded in synchronism. Fluffs and other errors can be corrected and an accurate match between words and pictures is assured because modern dubbing theatres are equipped with 'rock and roll', permitting film and soundtrack to be stopped at any convenient point without the loss of material already satisfactorily recorded. This is a tremendous advantage where lengthy or complicated sequences are concerned, and a direct contrast to the first dubbing theatre I ever used. There the only way of correcting a mistake was by going right back to the beginning.

recorded on to the sound track while the appropriate film is being shot. Thus, there is little room for error, either in the form and duration of each portion, or the reporter's delivery. Theoretically, all that remains after the processing stage is a simple task of assembly in the cutting room.

Film crews at work

Among all the people regularly engaged in routine television news work, members of film crews must be included among the most resourceful and energetic, rarely allowing themselves to be more than temporarily set back by the occasional failure of equipment or by the petty bureaucracies which beset so many news stories.

Crews frequently work on their own, without reporters or other editorial supervision of any kind and, as a result, have built up an undeniable roving independence envied by many. Partnerships between individual cameramen and recordists often last for years, the rapport between them occasionally developing to a point where their mutual understanding resembles the virtual telepathic state which exists in some good marriages.

As they work in so many different ways according to national custom it is impossible to generalise either about the standard film crew methods of operation or equipment used. But a fairly broad idea of both can be gained from the examination of a typical two-man crew working for BBC TV news in London.

First, transport. For all except foreign assignments, the team drive to every location in the car assigned to them as part of their equipment. This is usually one of the mass-produced saloons of the larger, more powerful variety, devoid of any special identification marks which might attract unwelcome attention. Apart from extra security locks for all doors and a radio-telephone link with base, the car is outwardly no different from any normal production-line model.

The only special requirement for a camera car is that it must have a spacious boot to accommodate all the equipment. This is carefully stowed away in four or five silver-coloured metal trunks robust enough to withstand the ill-treatment which is an inevitable part of the news-gathering process. The boxes are always unpacked and repacked by the crew with almost obsessional care, to a definite and unchanging pattern, so that there is a minimum delay before they are prepared for action.

As for the equipment itself, this varies from crew to crew depending to an extent on the magpie instincts of the individual. But it is likely to consist of most or all of the following:

One Arriflex BL or CP 16 sound camera (or equivalent) with 10:1 zoom lens.
Three or four 400 ft film magazines.
One 10 mm wide angle lens and holder.
One large lenshood.
6 ft extendible wooden tripod and case.
Two rechargeable battery packs with leads and shoulder straps.
One rechargeable battery belt.
One shoulder brace or chest harness as alternative to tripod.
One 6 ft extendible monopod as alternative to tripod.
One Uher or Nagra-type tape recorder for use independently or for operation of double system of film recording.
One mute camera—possibly a Bell & Howell Filmo with three-lens turret and clockwork-driven motor giving 30 sec. run.
Two exposure meters.
One miniature clapperboard and chalk.
One amplifier and cable for use with sound camera.
One close-up lens set.
Two neck microphones and cables.
One stick microphone and windshield.
One gun microphone and windbaffle.
One radio microphone and transmitter.
One black changing bag.
Two dozen self-adhesive labels.
One book of dopesheets and carbons.
Two dozen (onion) bags for dispatching film.
Tool kit.
Battery charger.
Three or four filters.
Ten rolls $\frac{1}{4}$ in tape in boxes.
Box of 18 spare batteries for tape recorder.
One battery-operated lighting unit.
Spare cable drum.
Ten 400 ft cans VNF 7240 (commag).
Ten 400 ft cans RT 400 (commag).
Ten 100 ft cans VNF 7240 (silent).

Ten 100ft cans RT 400 (silent).

Total value: approximately £16,000 (1978).

In addition, crews usually carry gum-boots, spare warm clothing and a small case containing passport, other personal documents, razor and spare shirts to meet unexpected foreign assignments.

Of the two roles, the cameraman's probably seems the most rewarding and inventive. It is he who usually places the camera into position, measures the light with an exposure meter, composes the picture and operates the camera. Sometimes, on routine assignments, he encourages his colleague to film under supervision, since this is probably the only way in which a recordist will gain enough experience to become a cameraman himself eventually.

The recordist is responsible for ensuring that the sound levels are correct and that the right microphone is chosen for the particular assignment. (See pages 143–144). He often doubles as magazine loader, focus-puller and chauffeur. When necessary he arranges for the despatch of the film. The recordist is also regarded as the team's main trouble-shooter, smoothing the ruffled brows of porters, commissionaires and any number of minor officials. It is often said that a recordist's ability to find the right palm to cross with silver frequently outweighs any shortcomings he might reveal as a technician. Be that as it may, it is clearly understood that the best film crew in the world are useless if they are stranded, unable to inveigle themselves and their equipment into the location to which they have been assigned.

As with other television news work, there are no rigid rules which camera crews ignore at their peril. So much depends upon time, place and type of story involved. All the same, there are a number of basic principles which the most conscientious crews have adopted and apply instinctively:

1. There is no substitute for a well-composed, sharp and rock-steady picture wherever possible. That means being exact in measuring the available light with an exposure meter and not only having a tripod or strong shoulder/chest harness as part of the equipment, but actually *using* it. Sudden jerking or shaking of the picture is entirely compatible with riots or other situations where the camera might have to be hand-

140

held; such movements are totally out of place in set-piece interviews conducted at relative leisure.

2. The leading film crews *always* use the sound channel on the sound camera, even though they may be recording only background noise. All appreciate that there is no such thing as complete silence, and that it is far easier to record the sound naturally at the time rather than add it in the dubbing theatre later on. It is amazing how even the most mundane, everyday sounds add an extra dimension to the simplest news stories.

3. It is a wise cameraman who acknowledges the need to keep the filming direct and straightforward. 'Arty' camerawork for its own sake is generally shunned. News filming means keeping out unnecessary pans, zooms and other movements, but also making sure that when they are used the ends of shots are held long enough for the film editor to 'get the scissors in' if he so desires. 'Hosepiping'—the rapid 'spraying' of the camera subject with the camera belongs to the world of the bad amateur home movie-maker rather than the television screen. But the professional cameraman also tries to avoid the boringly static scene which could just as well be captured by a still camera.

4. At all times, the best cameramen shoot their film with the cutting room in mind. They try to imagine how the film editor will set about assembling the material, and they produce plenty of variation in angles. Single, isolated shots are avoided, and efforts are taken to film in *sequences* of long shot, medium shot and close shot. Although cameramen are careful in their use of film, which is becoming an increasingly expensive commodity, it is false economy to restrict the material in such a way that makes the film editor's job impossible. Although some news cameramen pride themselves on having every usable foot of film transmitted (a ratio of 1 to 1), a more sensible aim would be 2 or 3 to 1, so that the film editor is not confined to assembling film to a strict pattern which allows no leeway.

Film equipment
Like so much else in television news, camera equipment has had to undergo radical and continuing development in order to keep

pace with the unending demands of the world news-gathering fraternity. In recent years manufacturers have largely succeeded in producing 16mm cameras which combine reliability and sturdiness without being too heavy, although physical strength remains an important asset for any cameraman who might be called on to carry around that solid lump of metal for hours at a stretch.

While a number of manufacturers continue to make the light, 16mm silent cameras for both professional and amateur use, the range of sound cameras for most news and documentary film work has been narrowed down to probably no more than three popular types. The *Arriflex BL*, made in West Germany, the American Cinema Products *CP 16* and the French *Eclair* are constructed for operation with either the single or double system of recording. All are driven by dry batteries which supply enough power for about 5000ft of film to be exposed before recharging becomes necessary.

Microphones. The choice of microphone is usually up to the sound recordist, the most efficient of whom carry a selection of types for use according to location and weather conditions.

For interviews in particular, sound recordists tend to favour the *neck microphone* (Fig. 34), otherwise referred to as a *personal*. This microphone is small, light, fastening easily round the neck, suspended by thin cord. Although it is not particularly obtrusive, some recordists like to hide the neck mike from the camera's view by slipping it under the coat worn by the user, while taking care to ensure that the speech is not muffled. As it is slung fairly near the mouth, the type is useful in some situations where the background noise is high, but it *is* sensitive to wind noise and crackles from the movement of nylon clothing or ties.

The second type in use is the *directional* or *gun mike*, (Fig. 35) aimed at the speaker by the recordist. It picks up sound over a long range, through a narrow angle, which enhances its versatility. But it is also inclined to restrict the cameraman, since the recordist or the microphone can easily creep into shot by mistake. The other genuine problem concerns the weapon-like outline of the microphone, which in some circumstances might draw dangerous attention to the user.

The third and possibly most used type is the simple *stick* microphone, (Fig. 36) held by the reporter rather than the recordist. It has no handling noise, can be prepared for use in a very short time, and has the extra benefit of giving the nervous or inexperienced

142

MICROPHONE TYPES

Fig. 34. Neck microphone. Useful for interviews where background noise is obtrusive. Picks up the crackle of nylon clothing or ties if put too close.

Fig. 35. All-purpose stick mike, easily made ready for action and used by reporter, it needs to be held firmly in the fist.

Fig. 36. Gun mike, held by sound recordist. Versatile but obtrusive, and dangerous in some situations because of its weapon-like outline.

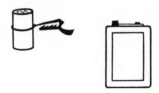

Fig. 37. Radio mike, excellent for lack of obtrusiveness, no wires being necessary. Neck-type mike can be clipped to clothing and the transmitter slips into the pocket. It is effective over several hundred yards' range.

reporter something useful to do with one of his hands. The stick mike should be grasped firmly near the top by the fist, not truncheon-like until the knuckles go white, or so delicately by the finger-tips that it waves about out of control. If used for inter-viewing it should be 'favoured' gently towards each speaker, preferably at an equal distance from every mouth to help the recordist keep sound levels balanced. It should *not* be thrust forward so aggressively that the speaker recoils in fear that it is about to be forced up his nose or down his throat. Although the stick mike remains rather ugly to look at, it is probably the best all-round microphone used for television news, especially with the addition of a foam shield to keep out wind noise. Nevertheless, like all the other types, it has the built-in disadvantage of allowing the reporter to be only as far away from the camera unit as the microphone lead and any extension will permit.

A fourth type, increasingly used by television news crews, gets over this inconvenience. This is the *radio* mike, which comes in two parts (Fig. 37); a neck-type microphone clips on to the cloth-ing or around the neck, and a transmitter slips into the reporter's pocket. It is possible to transmit over several hundred yards without the need for the umbilical cord connecting reporter to amplifier. Used sparingly, the radio mike is extremely effective, but some types are inclined to be temperamental and need to be treated with care, and that is not possible to guarantee in filming for news.

Other microphone types are rarely standard equipment but are sometimes available from a general pool. These include those fixed to booms above speakers' heads, and stand mikes, which are well known for producing high quality sound at the expense of obtrusiveness.

Lighting the set

Lighting assistants, otherwise known as *electricians* or '*sparks*', usually operate alone, independent of the news film units, as they are assigned only to those events, mostly at interior locations, where their services are known to be required.

In the back of their estate cars most carry up to four collapsible, free-standing lights of sufficient wattage to allow even exposure over an area equivalent to a medium-sized room measuring approximately 15 ft square. The necessary electrical current is obtained by tapping the normal domestic supply without any risk of overloading. Where no power source is available a small, hand-held battery light is used, but this is effective only over a very short range. Spare cable, bulbs, electrical sockets and plugs of every known shape and size make up the rest of the equipment, although many electricians, being as aquisitive as the camera crews, generally garner enough non-standard bits and pieces to meet most eventualities.

Many television journalists, including some with considerable experience, remain largely ignorant of the artificial lighting requirements for colour filming, and a few have been known to express pained surprise on discovering that news electricians do not normally travel with sufficient equipment to illuminate, without warning, areas as large as, say, the Royal Albert Hall or Madison Square Garden. Anything bigger than 15ft square calls for proper advance planning, some expense, and rather more manpower than a single electrician with four small lights.

Lighting as a career may not seem all that absorbing, but it does offer a unique position from which to observe news filming techniques at close quarters, and is often regarded by the ambitious as the first stepping stone along the way towards becoming a cameraman.

THE REPORTER ABROAD

FOR world television news services with internationally-minded audiences the task of covering important events in faraway places can be daunting, fraught with uncertainty and at times potentially crippling in expense. This means that while many of the less well-off are forced to rely on agency or pooled material picked up at relatively bargain-basement rates, the larger organisations, demanding exclusivity and speed, have no choice but to join the rat-race, praying that the budget will stand it and forever casting anxious glances over their shoulders to see how the rest of the competition is faring.

As a matter of priority, freelance contributors or resident staff on those foreign beats considered the most likely to produce a regular flow of broadcast material always establish their own local working arrangements and lines of communication. More severe examination of good organisation and logistical arrangements accompanies what are known as *fire brigade* operations, occasions when staff units are sent direct from home to cover specific stories for as long as they last.

Television news crews operate abroad under frequently untried conditions varying according to country and circumstance. Local attitudes range from enthusiasm, with an offer of every facility, through tolerance, to downright hostility leading to restriction of movement, harassment or arrest. "They say no foreign correspondent's training is complete until he has been arrested, and you get extra marks for being actually imprisoned or expelled . . ."[1] Even where there is a genuine readiness to co-operate, language barriers, unfamiliarity of terrain and a whole catalogue of major and minor differences provide their own natural obstacles in the path of efficient news-gathering. This does not

---

[1]John Timpson, *Today and Yesterday*, (George Allen & Unwin, 1976).

146

include making any allowances for the solution to the other, perhaps more important half of the equation—how to get the material on the air at home within scheduled programme times.

Three options suggest themselves. The first and most obvious is for the crew to collect all the material they have gathered and take it home at the end of the assignment. This may appear to be simple and foolproof, but 'hard' news has a notoriously short shelf-life, and the method is practicable only for the news-feature type of material, where the time-factor is not of overriding importance.

The second option, almost equally simple and obvious, is to send the film home by air as each separate stage of the assignment is completed. Part of every film crew's routine at any foreign destination is a thorough check of all airline flight times for the quickest and most direct routes home. Consequently, what appears on television screens around the world is unwittingly influenced to a surprising degree by those involved in the construction of flight timetables.

Over the years the actual business of '*shipping*' newsfilm has become a very much more established affair as airline staff employed in cargo departments find themselves handling increasing numbers of those precious 'onion' bags. Arrangements can even be made for the entire cost of shipment except local taxes to be met at the receiving end. All it requires at most friendly airports is enough time (sometimes no more than half an hour) before the flight in which to conclude the formalities of a customs declaration and to obtain a form of receipt called an *air waybill*. To speed clearance and collection at destination the waybill number is telephoned or telexed to those at home.

Scheduled passenger flights are not the only answer. Freighters and charters play their parts, too, and there are even rare occasions when the material is considered important enough for the news services themselves to hire their own aircraft to fly the film out.

An alternative to shipping film is *hand-carrying* it as the personal baggage of a member of the unit, air crew or cabin staff. On occasion the film is entrusted to a willing passenger, sometimes referred to as a *pigeon*, who is met on arrival by a representative of the news service in question and gratefully relieved of his burden. Although this method is employed frequently, and with success, it has always seemed to me to carry enormous risks. Having spent a large sum of money sending a film crew and equipment abroad, it would appear to be the height of folly to hand over a piece of valuable merchandise to a total stranger who, at the last moment, may have second thoughts about completing the errand. In these days of international terrorism, two or three hours aboard a crowded jet is rather too long a time to spend worrying whether the package thrust at you by an anxious-looking young man is as innocuous as he made you believe before he disappeared among the crowds at the airport terminal.

Even supposing this latest fact of modern life did not exist to deter all but the most accommodating traveller, there are enough stories about missed rendezvous to make the whole business of using a pigeon a fairly chancey one at the best of times.

So to the third option, open neither to the vagaries of the airline flight timetable nor to the whim of some fare-paying passenger. It is the fastest, dearest and most nerve-wracking method of all, employing the technical facilities of a local television station to send the film home direct via land links or communications satellites.

Despite the cost, this is the option being exercised more and more by the big news outfits with sophisticated audiences expecting same-day coverage of major events taking place virtually anywhere in the world.

It was the use of this option which began to change the face of television news in the late sixties and, as many would have it, helped shape the American people's ultimate attitude towards the war in Vietnam. Such a powerful phenomenon deserves closer examination.

Telling it to the birds

Sitting apparently motionless 22,300 miles above earth, a handful of man-made space stations are the agencies through which viewers of television news programmes are able to witness the momentous international events of their time—political changes, natural disasters, civil unrest, sport. And wars, of which Vietnam will go down in history as television's very first. It was the drip, drip of nightly newsfilm showing fighting in the jungle and paddy-fields which many believe finally sickened the American public into demanding an end to it all. Without the communications satellite to speed the coverage on its way between battlefront and living room, it is arguable whether the impact would have been as great, as soon. Vivid, full-colour pictures of this morning's fresh casualties have a gruesome reality that yesterday's somehow do not.

Throwing television pictures across continents is not, however, entirely new. Even in its formative days, BBC TV news managed to receive film direct from the United States using a BBC system known as *cablefilm*. This employed conventional transatlantic sound circuits, but it was an agonisingly slow process, requiring about an hour and a half for every minute of 16mm film. An extra hazard was that the sound had to be sent separately, making synchronisation another technical hurdle to be overcome before the whole could be transmitted.

The impetus for something faster and more reliable came, not surprisingly, from the Americans, who were already committed to the rapid development of space exploration. The principle was to bounce the picture and sound signals off orbiting satellites from one earth station to another.

The first satellite was launched, from Florida, in July 1962. This was a tiny piece of electronic wizardry called *Telstar*, a name soon to inspire a popular tune. Every two and a half hours it completed an orbit of the earth, each one bringing it within range of the three earth stations built in America, Britain and France. The immediate effect was sensational: the only trouble was that the satellite could be used for only a few minutes each orbit, at those times when it was visible to both sides of the Atlantic.

Within a very short time Telstar had proved to be only the fore-runner of a world-wide satellite system for public use. This was the International Telecommunications Satellite Organisation, more generally known as Intelsat, formed in August, 1964, with a founder membership of 19 countries.

The first satellite launched under the Intelsat umbrella was *Early Bird*, in 1965. Although it was capable of providing only one television channel for use between Europe and North America, this 85-pound satellite has won a permanent place in the vocabulary of television news journalists. To this day, satellites are known as 'Birds', and 'Birding' has become the accepted term for the entire process of satellite transmission of news.[1]

Early Bird, otherwise known as *Intelsat I*, was followed over the

---

[1] Early Bird, with an original design life of 18 months, went on operating continuously for three and a half years.

next five years by bigger and better satellites, three *Intelsat II*, five *Intelsat III*. And as these, too, ended their useful lives, their places were taken by seven satellites in an *Intelsat IV* series, the first of which was launched in 1971, and others in the even more sophisticated *Intelsat IV-A* series, four years later.

By the beginning of 1978 the service to the countries of the global system was being shared by a total of seven of these two newer types, with three positioned over the busy Atlantic Ocean Region and two each over the Indian and Pacific Oceans. Each one is either fully operational or standing by to cover break-downs or sudden extra demand, and appears to be stationary in its appointed place above the equator, not only picking up and re-transmitting the signals but amplifying them as well.

Work on a further generation of satellites better equipped to meet the demands of the early nineteen-eighties, is already under way. Seven *Intelsat V* satellites, each with a communications capacity equivalent to 12,000 simultaneous telephone conversations and two television channels (about double that of the *Intelsat IV-A*) are planned, the first due for launching towards the end of 1979.

The construction of earth stations to send and receive the signals has also been continuing apace. By the end of 1977 there were 163 of them, compared with only five at the time of *Early Bird*.

The Intelsat organisation itself now has more than a hundred member countries, most of which are represented by their national telecommunications enterprises. Each pays towards operating costs, research and development in proportion to the use it makes of the system. The United States, as the biggest investor, runs Intelsat on behalf of all the other members through COMSAT, the Communications Satellite Organisation. Satellites are launched from Florida, on the south coast, by NASA, the National Aeronautics and Space Administration, which was also responsible for the Apollo moon-landing and associated space programmes. It has not been an entirely unblemished record of success. Some satellites failed to reach their correct orbits and others were lost when the launch vehicles went wrong.

Not surprisingly, the vast sums involved in establishing and developing the system have led, in turn, to high tariffs for the users. As an example, a European service renting the television circuits of an Intelsat satellite for the minimum booking time of ten minutes pays 1780 dollars from New York or Washington at peak time, plus 58 dollars for each subsequent minute.[1] These costs, which do not include the use of facilities provided by local television stations, can, however, be split between any number of organisations. When three or more agree to share the same material the transmission is known as a *multilateral* feed.[2] Where *Unilateral* (ie exclusive) use is demanded the hirer bears the whole amount. Since cancellation charges are also high, even the most affluent television organisations tend to look hard at their news judgement before committing themselves to booking unilateral satellite time.

The establishment of circuits between two continents for satellite transmission purposes is now a daily occurrence. The administrative and technical procedure can be completed in a very short time, probably within the hour when necessary, which means that major, late-breaking news stories can usually be accommodated.

Those responsible for harvesting international news believe that the satellite system, sophisticated as it is as present, is still in its infancy. John Heuston, foreign news editor of the BBC, is not alone in believing that the day is not too far off when countries will be able to beam material into space for storage in satellite memory banks. Then the touch of a computer button by a television journalist on the other side of the world will be sufficient to produce, at the most suitable moment, a selection from the catalogue of electronic news.

The little matter of how all the circuits are knitted together is usually far from the mind of the fireman-reporter, much more concerned with meeting the deadline for his satellite transmission into a news programme several thousand miles and time zones away. Fine calculations on the spot are required every time to ensure that not only is the news material itself safely gathered in (surprisingly, sometimes the most simple part of the exercise), but that the film is returned from location in sufficient time to complete all the other processes before that ten-minute 'window' opens and closes for good.

That, of course, is on the assumption that all the necessary arrangements have been made in advance. There is no point in

---

[1] 1977 prices. 'Cheap Rate' (about half-price) transmission from America is available between early morning and lunch-time, GMT.
[2] Other forms of cost-reducing include the *bilateral* (two-way split) and the *sequential unilateral* (exclusive use of circuits already established for another organisation same geographical area).

booking satellite time for a five-minute studio/film package unless processing, editing, telecine and studio are all known to be ready and waiting. There is no point in arriving with hundreds of feet of the most exciting newsfilm shot on a stock which the local processing plant cannot handle and no point at all in turning up in great haste at a heavily-guarded television station without some form of acceptable documentation or at least the correct name of the present local coordinator. Trying to explain to a soldier with an itchy trigger finger on a sub-machine gun that it has all been arranged 'by the office', and would he please stand aside to let you, your two colleagues, a large hire-car and a third of a ton of film equipment inside at once is not the most enviable task to be faced with in a foreign country. The arrangements may indeed have been made by the office, but the office is a good three thousand miles away, and what may have seemed like a firm promise made to them at high level over the telex yesterday turns out to be a commitment to provide every facility *tomorrow*. *Today* is a national holiday and a skeleton staff only is on duty.

Even assuming that all does go according to plan, in unfamiliar surroundings, with local technicians perhaps not fired by the same enthusiasm and urgency, the reporter finds the hours towards transmission appearing to melt away at a disconcerting rate. Distances between different departments seem to grow further apart, each stage in the process proceeds at little better than a snail's pace, accompanied by a lengthy and seemingly irrelevant discussion in a language not the reporter's own, until the sickening realisation dawns that now only minutes remain and the last joins in the film have yet to be made. For the reporter and film crew, on whom the news team at home are depending so much, the tension becomes almost unbearable. Will that effort be wasted, after all, in the dreadful anti-climax of a missed deadline? Fortunately, persistence and a refusal to panic under even such circumstances have a tendency to pay off.

All in all, a remarkable spirit of professional cooperation exists between television stations of different countries, not for purely altruistic reasons alone, but a sound, practical one. The hosts today may find themselves the guests tomorrow, the day after, or at any rate the day after that, in maybe almost identical circumstances.

Working through Eurovision
In Europe, the provision of unilateral facilities by members of

the *European Broadcasting Union* for television newsmen from other countries is only half the story. The other is made up by the *Eurovision News Exchange*, the model on which many other similar organisations have been built elsewhere.

The Eurovision News Exchange has been called a clearing house for television news—an electronic market-place through which this much sought-after commodity can pass unhindered across the frontiers of member countries.

Three times a day, news items of European interest are fed into the network of land lines for use by the news services, any of whom, in theory, are thus able to receive a complete portfolio of foreign coverage without the expense of originating their own. The only costs involved are for a share of the circuits, the actual amount of payment being calculated on the number of television sets in use in the receiving country.

The original and still valid concept of Eurovision was based on the common interest which exists between television news audiences of different nationalities. For the journalists, there were several attractions. First, those already committed to covering an event for a domestic programme would undoubtedly be willing to make the same material available to others later, as long as this did not jeopardise their own television news. Secondly, there was an accepted principle of reciprocity. Thirdly, coverage by people on the spot was bound to be available relatively quickly. And fourthly, the need to send staff crews abroad to cover 'borderline' stories would become unnecessary.

So after successful trials in the late fifties, the Eurovision News Exchange was born in May 1961, beginning with a transmission at five o'clock, central European time, every afternoon. Seven years later, the first news exchange took on the title of EVN-1 when it was supplemented by a second, EVN-2, transmitted at five minutes to seven. A third, EVN-0, with transmission at mid-day, was added in March 1974, to serve the increasing number of lunch-time news programmes. Extra, unexpected items of major importance are sometimes offered outside the regular exchanges as 'flashes' or extracts from other news programmes as they are transmitted. Depending on the events of the day, the duration of each transmission varies, but EVN-1 is invariably the longest, coinciding as it does with most of the early-evening news bulletins in Europe, and EVN-2 the shortest.

Until a few years ago, the exchanges were the almost exclusive preserves of the member news services themselves. Since then the major agencies, CBS, UPITN and Visnews have begun to make increasingly big contributions between them, passing the fifty per cent mark for the first time in 1973.[1]

The items to be exchanged are sent in turn from each originating country, all routed through the Eurovision technical centre in Brussels. There is a separate administrative set-up in Geneva, headquarters of the European Broadcasting Union, and an office in New York, opened in 1970 to co-ordinate satellite transmissions between North America and Europe.

The content of each daily exchange is decided at an early-morning editorial conference conducted over the network sound link. The chairman, called the *news co-ordinator*, is drawn from each member country in rotation and presides for ten-day spells from a microphone at home base.

Business proceeds at a brisk pace in the two working languages of English and French. An offer to provide an item of coverage has to be accepted by a minimum of two services before it can be included in the 'running order' for any of the exchanges. Sometimes members express interest in events not being offered by the country concerned, in which case an offer may or may not be forthcoming later on. Confirmation of all offers and acceptances is made by telex after the conference, when participants have had the opportunity of further editorial discussions at home.

Ten minutes before the beginning of EVN-0 and EVN-2 the sound circuits are re-established so that final details of content and duration can be passed on before items are recorded on to videotape. The half hour allowed before EVN-1 is used partly to discuss possible coverage for next day.[2/3]

The fixer

With the creation of such sophisticated clubs as Eurovision, the parallel growth of unilateral coverage using other peoples' technical facilities has given birth to a new breed of television journalist, known as the *fixer*. Crude though this title may be, it does accurately convey the essence of the task, as a member of the 'fire brigade' team to fix the many loose ends at the scene of a major news event so that transmission into bulletins at home by satellite or land line can proceed with the minimum of difficulty.

The fixer's duties are based on the fact that the reporter/ correspondent and film crew covering any news story are capable of being in only one place at a time, either out in the thick of the action on location or back at the local television station, negotiating over such small, time-consuming but significant matters as the allocation of a cutting room. It is this kind of detail which comes within the orbit of the fixer, and so leaves the rest of the team free to concentrate on their own particular problems in the field. As a bonus, the fixer is there to supervise the editing, write or advise on the script and soothe the anxieties of those at home by providing frequent progress reports by telex or telephone.

Therefore the fixer needs to be of some editorial seniority, trusted for his judgement, and the possessor of a sound enough knowledge of all the television techniques to be able to cut corners in a crisis. The work is sometimes boring, sitting about for hours in a foreign television station far from where important things are happening, frequently testing—trying to persuade a disinterested local laboratory crew to process your film before your national rivals', but almost always worthwhile.

Assignments, usually given on a temporary, story-by-story basis, are much sought after, particularly when they involve foreign travel[4] and the glamour scarcely seems to pall even though the most important task of one whole trip might be no more creative than jumping in a taxi to take one hundred feet of film to a commercial laboratory miles away because the only other colour processing plant in the country has broken down.

---

[1] Approximately 3,000 separate items out of just under a total 6,000 transmitted. (Source—*EBU Review*, May 1975).

[2] For more detailed accounts of the working of Eurovision see *The Universal Eye, World Television in the Seventies*, by Timothy Green (The Bodley Head, 1972) and *The TV News Exchange* (EBU Review, May 1975.)

[3] Eurovision has regular links with other international networks including Intervision, the system established by the Prague-based International Radio and Television Organisation (OIRT) in January, 1960. The Intervision News Exchange (IVN), was set up in May, 1964, and consisted at first of a weekly transmission every Friday afternoon at two fifteen, Central European Time. Within five years this had been extended to an exchange every day except Sunday and the time of transmission put back to four o'clock to enable more up-to-date material to be sent in time for members' early evening programmes. Other developments have since included the introduction of a Sunday exchange (1970) and the inclusion of colour (1971). IVN has seven regular participants—the television services of Bulgaria, Czechoslovakia, East Germany, Hungary, Poland, Rumania and the Soviet Union—with Austria, Finland and Yugoslavia (all members of the Eurovision network) also supplying material from time to time. Altogether, the number of IVN items transmitted has grown considerably, from about 500 in the first year of operation, to 4,672 in 1976, although the amount of material accompanied by natural sound was still below fifty per cent. (Source: OIRT).

[4] The practice of sending fixers on domestic stories is also growing; some news services also send their own film editors out with field teams.

CONSTRUCTING A NEWS PROGRAMME

FASHIONS change in television news just as much as they do in any other walk of life. The BBC's idea back in July 1954, when it decided to replace a highly popular, cinema-style nightly 'newsreel' was that of a disembodied voice reading solemnly over a succession of agency photographs and maps, followed (at a respectful distance) by a series of film clips strung together.

Although the exercise was greeted with minimal enthusiasm by the critics, viewers in those innocent days were a good deal less demanding. To them, every programme was still practically an adventure, and the fact that some more-or-less up to date film appeared on the news was often regarded as being of greater significance than its actual relevance to the day's events. Neither had television yet begun to exert its influence as a major medium of information.

Today's audience is far more discerning, with the same high standards of presentation and production expected of the news as of any programme which might have taken months rather than hours to prepare. Because television news cannot appear to be lagging behind in professional gloss or technical excellence the journalists have been drawn (perhaps a little reluctantly) by the need to produce not just news *on* television but news *for* television.

The list of unrelated events has gone, to be replaced by *programmes*, thoughtfully constructed, prettily packaged. Designers are brought in to sweat over new opening and closing sequences and the occasional change of set. Formats are entirely revamped; old faces disappear, new ones take over. However much the old news hands may deplore it, the public has come to expect an element of 'show biz' about the nightly news, even it it is confined to the window-dressing at the end, when the presenters relax, smile, ostentatiously finger their scripts and exchange pleasantries for viewers' benefit.

These visual trimmings are important. Just as a newspaper seeks to attract its readers with the layout of its pages and its typographical styles as much as with the quality of its content, so the television news programme has to find a way of capturing audience interest and holding on to it right through to the end twenty-five or thirty minutes later. Now, even more than ever before, audiences are being asked to grasp complex and abstract matters which have a direct bearing on their lives. They have no chance of understanding any of them unless the subjects are presented clearly and unambiguously.

There is, however, one overriding factor. Duration. Television news comes in all shapes and sizes, ranging from all-vision summaries lasting a minute or two to the marathon feasts mounted by American networks. And, like it or not, duration has a fundamental influence on style. The shorter the programme the shorter the individual items within it, the less room for frills, with only the bare bones of the day's news capable of being squeezed in. The longer the programme the greater the opportunity to cast the net more widely, employing the full panoply of television techniques.

But how long is a long programme? Some say that even the half-hour news, so much the pattern in many parts of the world, is insufficient in which to communicate anything except the essentials. They also complain that television editors, faced with a choice between spending reasonable time on a few items told in detail and many given in brief, tend to opt for quantity. In Britain the argument has been put forward that viewers are not given nearly enough explanation to go with the information, and that individual stories are not dealt with at anything like their 'proper' length (whatever that is). This, in turn, has led to what has been termed a 'bias against understanding'. The basis of the charge is that most events form part of a continuing process and therefore cannot be dealt with in isolation. Britain's economic problems, it is said, manifest themselves in a wide variety of symptoms including deterioration in the balance of payments, rising unemployment, accelerating inflation and so on.

The news, "devoting two minutes on successive nights to the latest unemployment figures, or the state of the stock market, with no time to put the story in context, gives the viewer no sense of how many of these problems relate to each other. It is more likely to leave him confused and uneasy."[1]

According to Robin Day, apart from the main stories, "the items dealt with in brief are so baldly summarised that the meaning may not be apparent until one reads a newspaper in the morning."[2] Day goes on to argue the case for an hour of news on British television—a kind of newspaper of the screen, to include expanded coverage in 'specialist' areas such as sport, industry, education, science and so on.

All this assumes that the public actually wants more news on television: there are those who would say that there is already too much. Ordinary television journalists are not among them, of course. But while every serious-minded news practitioner is always eager to put forward sound reasons for more and longer programmes (together with enough extra money to finance them) the honest ones are equally prepared to admit the truth, that in the crowded world of television programming, news is only one tenant. Drama, entertainment, education and the rest have to live in it too, and it would be entirely wrong of journalists to lose sight of the fact that, however much it hurts, *they* have to fit in with the schedules, not the other way round.

Still, the journalist has some consolation in the knowledge that he is not operating in a vacuum. If he genuinely believes in the importance of communicating current events to a wide public he will rejoice that others are sharing the burden. Although it may well have been proved beyond doubt that more people obtain their information from television than from any other source, it is equally true that television is not and cannot be the sole provider. Radio, newspapers and magazines all have their own special contributions to make towards the sum total of knowledge, and it would be foolish as well as arrogant for the television newsman to suggest otherwise.

The supreme test, therefore, must lie in the use of available air time to present the news attractively as well as intelligently. Stories which are well chosen in the first place, then carefully written and edited to present the most important facts with the utmost clarity and simplicity are perfectly capable of conveying the message, even in a short time. There is no point whatever in assaulting the viewer with irrelevancies and repetitions masquerading under the name of depth, when all they really do is add

---

[1] John Birt, head of Current Affairs, London Weekend Television, in *The Times*, February 28, 1975.
[2] Robin Day, *Day by Day: a Dose of My Own Hemlock*. (William Kimber, 1975.)

length. One of the skills fundamental to all forms of journalism is the ability to make selection. To run every interview in full is to abdicate editorial responsibility.

Putting it together

In the past, much television news was so short that editors preferred not to waste even a few seconds in reciting the contents. These followed soon enough anyway, items crowding one upon another, unannounced, at breakneck speed, more or less in order of importance. If bulletins looked like overrunning, cuts could then be made from the bottom up without seeming to disturb such overall shape as there was.

Since air-time has become more generous, this philosophy has been made to seem out of date. In its place has evolved the concept of television news as a programme, dependent for its success on the ability of those in charge to take a series of disparate events and fashion them into something with a recognisable outline of its own.

The criticism is made that in reaching out for that goal, editors sometimes allow themselves to be over-influenced by the availability of pictures. Such a generalisation is impossible to prove one way or the other. Yet, if it is true, there seems little shame in admitting it: by what other criterion should a medium which deals in pictures base its judgements? Given a reasonable alternative, no editor would choose to open a peak-time television news programme with an indigestible wad of vision stories and studio spots, leaving the first piece of film until ten minutes have passed. It has never meant ignoring the important non-visual in favour of the trivial pictorial. What it does mean is encouraging editors to apply to television news the values of television, as opposed to those of newspapers or radio. Ninety-nine times out of a hundred they will be the same. When they are not, editors are expected to beg to differ and go all out to exploit the advantage they have over the printed word.

In many ways the argument is not so much about what constitutes a 'good story' as about emphasis. On a front page of a newspaper, clever layout is used to direct the reader's eye quickly to the most important story, or to any one of a number given equal prominence. In television news, the implication is that importance is synonymous with the order in which events are transmitted.

In reality, whether or not they always succeed, some television news editors would rather concentrate on producing programmes which viewers find easy to follow. Instead of being sprinkled haphazardly throughout a programme like confetti, stories are sorted into small groups. An item about domestic industrial output, for example, might lead logically to one about exports, which puts the audience into a receptive frame of mind for a report from abroad. Brick-by-brick the programme edifice is built up in this way—little sequences of events linked together by association of subject, geography, or both. Individual durations and treatments have to be considered in parallel, the result of which leads to some stories being detached from one group to join another, or made to stand in isolation. There is no virtue in constructing a tortuous link for its own sake, or in 'promoting' a story far beyond its importance just because it seems to fit. Without making a fetish of it, the target is to produce a programme which looks as though some thought and care has been given to its construction.

An essential part of the formula has been added with an innovation known as the *menu* or *headline sequence*, which summarises each outstanding item in the programme, often in no more than a single sentence, so that impatient viewers are not forced to wait until events unfold before them. Over the years, the headlines have developed from being straightforward reads in or out of vision, into proper sequences in their own right, with combinations of stills, captions, film and videotape extracts to whet the appetite.

As well as imparting urgency at the top of the programme, the headline technique has added a previously unknown degree of flexibility. Once the bald details have been given, there is no rule to say that the full reports themselves must follow each other in a block, or indeed, in the same order. Instead, editors have begun to enjoy a freedom to distribute their ration of 'goodies' at points which help news programmes to achieve pace, variety and balance.

At the same time, other options have presented themselves to editors and producers eager for some format which will enable their programmes to stand out. Ideas are tried and discarded, varied and tried again. New questions arise . . . whether there should be one newsreader per programme or two . . . whether studio introductions to films should be read by one person, out-of-vision commentaries by another . . . what kind and colour of background should be used—a plain, pastel studio wall, some

160

illustration changing to suit each story, or just a static programme symbol . . . whether correspondents or reporters appearing in vision in the studio should be given the same backgrounds as the newsreaders . . . whether opening and closing title sequences should be accompanied by music or sound effects . . . whether there should even *be* set titles instead of something which changes daily according to programme content . . . whether each particpant in the programme should be introduced by name orally or by means of a superimposition on the screen . . . whether the newsreader should preface the first story with a "Good morning" or "Good evening" or plunge straight into the day's news . . . whether studio performers should be framed dead-centre or offset to one side of the screen. All this, and much more has to be decided with as much care and consideration as the way the news itself is to be reported. For without being offered an attractive wrapping, the audience may not wait to examine the contents.

Programme running order

An 'act of faith' is how a senior BBC colleague once described the production process of every television news programme—faith in the certainty that each separate member of the news team is carrying out his allotted task while everyone else is doing the same. It is a faith which permeates work on the road, in the newsroom, in the cutting rooms, in the videotape suites and in the studios. And the basis of it is good communication, oral or written, without which, in the continually shifting sands of news, the whole thing would promptly collapse.

To the uninitiated, the daily home and foreign news diaries, the 'prospects' setting out details of coverage, the wall-charts on which completed assignments are ticked off, probably seem confusing and unnecessary. To those engaged on the serious business of constructing something tangible out of hopes, promises and expectations, they represent a comforting reminder of the vast amount of effort being expended for the sake of a common goal.

The contribution of the output editorial staff is known as the *running order*, on which is listed not only the sequence of stories to be transmitted, but also how the separate elements used in each item, newsreader, stills, charts, film and so on, are intended to contribute towards the broadcast as a whole. Without that information to go by, the production staff would be totally at a

161

loss, unable to assemble the relevant technical facilities at the required moment during transmission.

While practical necessity demands that the running order be drawn up and widely distributed at least an hour beforehand, chances are that it will be subjected to considerable change before transmission. So much of what is committed firmly to paper is educated guesswork, based on frequently sketchy information about estimated times of arrival of film and videotape items and the notional times needed for processing, editing and scripting.

But the running order is the foundation on which the programme begins to assume a definite shape. It is usually put together at an editorial conference presided over by the editor for the day who (with or without canvassing colleagues for their opinions) outlines the framework and gives an idea of the approximate time he or she proposes to devote to the separate programme segments. Each item is given a page number and title by which it is identified throughout its brief life to avoid any possible confusion in the frantic last few minutes before transmission. Where stories are particularly complex, or have several strands to them, they are allocated successive page numbers and titles. This is so that the writers responsible can get scripts typed page by page to speed distribution.

Running orders also contain several numbers against which there are no titles. This is to make allowance for any new stories to be slotted in without disturbing everything else. Where really drastic changes cannot be accommodated the whole sheet may have to be scrapped and re-written. Any changes, no matter how small, have to be communicated to the production staff, so that by the time the broadcast begins no one involved is left in doubt about the part he is expected to play.

The running order layout itself is important, although it does not have to be complicated. The chief consideration is for it to be easily understood. Essential ingredients are numbers, titles and sources:

THE FIVE O'CLOCK REPORT   *Running Order*
Monday, January 14.   Studio Two.   Rehearsal 4.25 p.m.
Director: Bert Brown   Newsreader: Phil Jones
CAPTION TITLES AND SIGNATURE TUNE (15″)

1. MENU   PHIL/STILLS
2.

```
 3.
 4. PRIME MINISTER          PHIL
 5. P.M./INTERVIEW          FILM
 6. P.M./REACTION           PHIL/STILLS
 7. P.M./POLITICAL          INJECT (ex Parl't)
 8.
 9.
10. STRIKE                  PHIL
11. STRIKE/LIBRARY          FILM
12. STRIKE/IAN              SS (CSO factory)
13. STRIKE/PAY OFF          PHIL
14.
15. FACTORY FIRE            PHIL/MAP
16. FIRE/MIDLANDS           VT/SUPERS
17.
18. COLLISION               PHIL/MAP
19. COLLISION/CHANNEL       FILM
20.
21. PARIS DEMO              PHIL
22. PARIS/EVN               VT
23. MOSCOW PARADE           VT
24. U.S. PRESIDENT          STILL
25.
26. RABIES SCARE            PHIL
27. MILK                    PHIL/CHART
28. MILK/TOPFIELD FARM      FILM/SUPERS
29.
30.
31. AIR FARES               PHIL/CHARTS
32. NEW PLANE               PHIL
33. PLANE/REPORT            FILM/SUPERS
34. PLANE/ADD               PHIL
35.
36.
37.
38. LA SALVA COUP           PHIL/MAP/STILLS
39. LA SALVA/HARRIS         TAPE/STILL/SUPER
40. LA SALVA/BRITON         PHIL
41. LA SALVA/INTERVIEW      VT/SUPER
42.
43.
44. MISSING PAINTINGS       PHIL/STILL
```

45.	
46. BABY	PHIL
47. BABY/HOSPITAL	FILM (2ND VOICE?)
48. BABY/STEWARDESS	FILM/SUPER
49. BABY/ADD	PHIL
50.	
51. ENGLAND TEAM	PHIL/CHART/STILLS
52.	
53. MARATHON	PHIL
54. MARATHON MAN	VT
55.	
56. WEIGH-IN	PHIL
57. WEIGH-IN/TODAY	FILM
58.	
59.	
60. END HEADS	PHIL/TAPE/CAPTION

Behind what may seem to be a straightforward enough exercise, a great depth of journalistic experience and understanding has to be shown by the editor in the hours between the daily round of conferences and the drawing up of the running order.

In this example of the fictitious 'Five O'clock Report', it is quite possible to imagine that several diary stories have not come up to expectations and have had to be discarded. Suggestions for coverage of a handful of new, 'borderline' stories have been weighed then rejected; a special film report from one of the staff foreign correspondents has failed to arrive in time for the programme and the extra news agency stories put forward by the copytaster for possible use all turn out to offer no advance on what is already in hand.

Much of what is listed for inclusion is as predicted, and the one remaining doubt in the editor's mind is whether to begin the programme with something which *was* unexpected—an early-morning explosion and fire at a factory two hundred miles away. Two people are known to have died, not a great loss of life, but factory safety is at present a matter of great public concern and staff from the regional newsroom, quick off the mark, are at work putting together what seems to be an excellent account of the accident, with pictures and interviews. To add to that, a collision between two foreign ships a few miles off the coast, with a possibility that up to eight crew members have been killed, makes the temptation to lead with the double disaster a considerable one.

Instead, with a certain amount of reluctance, the editor decides to give pride of place to the Prime Minister's forecast that the economic crisis might be coming to an end. A statement along these lines has been expected for some days, but it has now come out in a rather less cautious form than the political correspondent had been led to believe. The Prime Minister's willingness to be interviewed on the subject is also a factor. So economics find their way to the top of the news, the sequence completed with reaction from opposing politicians and a live report from parliament by the political correspondent to put everything into perspective.

The economic theme is continued by reporting the strike at a factory which makes components for the motor industry. It is significant because it could lead to lay-offs, affecting in turn exports and the Prime Minister's hoped-for economic revival. The industrial correspondent is expected to return in time from a meeting between the government's arbitration service, management and union, from which it is hoped some news of a settlement may emerge. It means a second correspondent appearing in the studio high up in the programme, but since both stories do really seem to need authoritative explanation, the editor decides there is no alternative.

With the economy out of the way, the reports of the two accidents can come next. On sheer number of casualties alone, the ship collision ought to merit the higher place in the running order. But there are other factors to be considered. First, the factory explosion is domestic and has potentially serious ramifications, while the collision seems to have been the result of a simple navigational error in fog. Second, there is full coverage of the factory disaster, but the visual material available on the other story is expected to consist of no more than a minute of film, taken from the air, of one of the damaged vessels under tow. Third, and decisively, the incident at sea makes a far neater transition from a sequence of 'home' stories to a sequence of 'foreign' ones. These concern a workers' demonstration in Paris and a military parade in Moscow (both offered on the Eurovision News Exchange) and comments made by the United States President about future East-West relations.

The editor did wonder whether to extend the foreign sequence with a report of a military take-over in a small but important South American republic, especially as some impressive stills

165

have come over the wire and there is a telephoned dispatch from the local correspondent. Eventually, he decides to save the item for the latter half of the programme, which is looking distinctly thin without the substantial foreign film report which went astray in transit and won't arrive until tomorrow.

Casting around for something with which to 'come home' after the foreign sequence, the editor puts in a brief vision story about a tourist thought to have been bitten by a rabid dog during a continental camping holiday, and follows it with the embargoed announcement of a rise in milk prices. That, and the connecting Topfield Farm film, were at one time considered as a strong second story before the strike, but after some discussion, the editor decided it would have made the programme look rather top-heavy. So now it comes about halfway through. A proposed new structure for domestic air fares seems to follow naturally, and that coincides with film of the maiden flight of a revolutionary new passenger aircraft.

From there, the programme takes an entirely new direction with the South American coup report, which is rounded off with an interview with a businessman who returned from the country only the day before the take-over. A vision and still story about some stolen valuable paintings acts as a useful buffer in front of a good 'human interest' tale about a baby girl born prematurely in mid-flight over the Atlantic. There are good pictures of the child in an oxygen tent in hospital, and an interview with the stewardess who helped deliver her. The editor spotted the possible link between this story and the plane report, but decides to ignore it.

Towards the end, after the ritual announcement of an England cricket touring team, are two more lightweight sport items. The editor hopes that the rest of the programme will come out at sufficient length to enable him to discard one of these two stories but, for the time being, uncertainty about the duration of the factory explosion report has forced him to include both.

To close the programme there is the usual recap of the main points of the news, and the closing titles.

An alternative to the formal running order is to leave the final permutation until shortly before transmission. Although this method is known to work perfectly well under some circumstances, it does seem to introduce another, unnecessary element of uncertainty into a process which is already fraught with difficulty. I would hesitate to recommend the practice for any except the least intricate programmes.

Setting out the script

Hand-in-hand with the numbered running order goes the need for carefully setting out every page of script. This discipline is perhaps not needed where very small staff are concerned, but big news and production teams, particularly those operating on shift-working lines, need to conform to a 'house' style readily understood and accepted by everyone.

Just as the running order dictates what elements the programme contains, the written script influences how and when they are introduced. The studio director, glancing at a fresh page arriving in the control gallery two minutes before air-time, must be able to feel confident that following its instructions without hesitation will not lead to disaster. Poor typing or idiosyncratic lay-out could easily lead to misunderstandings among the production staff, with chaotic results.

The scripts themselves are usually typed by trained staff working alongside the journalists in the newsroom. By convention, each page is typed in nothing less than double spacing, technical and production instructions being given on the left-hand side, dialogue or commentary on the right. Numbers and titles must correspond with those given on the running order, and the duration of separate components added to help those constructing the programme keep in step with overall length. Production staff, too, rely on these timings so that new sources can be introduced into the programme at the exact moment they are required.

The number of script copies required for each programme must depend on the number of people involved with production. In some cases half a dozen may be sufficient, turned out by the writers themselves using typewriters with jumbo-sized lettering. In others, forty or more may have to go round. My own view is that despite the rising cost of paper it is far better to have too many script copies than too few.

One more thought. Some services making several transmissions a day give each programme its own paper colour code. In that way there is no chance of a spare page left over from, say, the afternoon news, creeping into the late evening programme by mistake.

This is how the opening few pages of The Five O'Clock Report might be set out:

---

5 O'Clock Report   MENU   Mon. Jan. 14

CAPTION TITLES & SIG. TUNE (15″)

STILL 1 (P.M.) ——————— The Prime Minister says
the economic crisis may
be coming to an end.

STILL 2 (BODY) ——————— At least ten people die
in two disasters—a
collision at sea and a
fire at a Midlands factory.

STILL 3 (PLANE)——————— A revolutionary new
passenger plane takes to
the air for the first time.

STILL 4 (BABY) ——————— And we take a look at
the baby girl born
this morning aboard a
transatlantic jet.

15″ (TITLES)+20″

5 O'Clock Report　　　PRIME MINISTER　　　Mon. Jan. 14

PHIL IN VISION ———————— The Prime Minister says he
thinks the economic crisis
may be nearing an end. He
told MPs this afternoon
that the balance of payments
has improved so much, all
the indications are that it
won't be long before there's
a healthy surplus. But he's
also warned against complacency.
There is, he says, still a
difficult time ahead for
everyone. John Jennings asked
him if he wasn't being too
optimistic about the future.

FILM FOLLOWS

24″

5 O'Clock Report   P.M./INTERVIEW   Mon. Jan. 14

FILM (1′ 28″)

SPEECH BEGINS: ——— "No, not this time . . ."

SPEECH ENDS: ——— ". . . I wouldn't like people to think that."

1′ 28″ (FILM)

—6—

5 O'Clock Report   P.M./REACTION   Mon. Jan. 14

PHIL IN VISION ——— The immediate reaction from the Leader of the Opposition was one of disbelief.

STILL 1 (JONES) ——— Mr Albert Jones said the Prime Minister was deluding himself and the country if he really thought the worst was over. And.

STILL 2 (SMITH) ——— Mrs Aga Smith, for the National Nonconformists, said any improvement was probably more to do with the recovery of world trade than successful Government policies.

20″

—7—

As can be seen from the examples, the production instructions are strictly limited.

PHIL IN VISION

does not go on to say *how* the shot of Phil should be framed; the instruction when to introduce the

STILL

goes no further than identifying the subject. The rest is left to the discretion of the studio director and the production team, although sensible suggestions of where electronic mixes, wipes or other production techniques might add something to the presentation will probably be carried out if the writer has taken the trouble to include them.

Directors of some news services prefer their scripts to contain much more technical information to differentiate between the types of stills (prints or slides) and films (mute, commag or sepmag) in use. There are also variations in terminology of command from

TAKE FILM

or

TAKE TC (Telecine)

to

TAKE SOF (Sound on film).

Uniformity might be considered ideal, but as long as the staff concerned understand what is required of them, it hardly seems important.

PRODUCTION AND PRESENTATION

Control room

LIKE the bridge of a modern supertanker or the cockpit of a long-range jet, the control gallery of a television studio is a world of its own, dominated by electronic gadgetry of seemingly overwhelming proportions. It is cramped, dim and claustrophobic. The main source of light comes from a bank of television monitors which reflect the seeing eyes of the cameras in the brightly-lit studio next door. Other small squares of light shine from the illuminated buttons on control panels, at which sit shadowy figures, heads bent over scripts. Tension and excitement lie close beneath the surface air of calm efficiency.

This, then, is the nerve centre of a television news broadcast, the one and only place at which the editorial function (supreme until now) has to take second place. For this is the moment when the production team and engineers hold sway as they set about the intricacies of translating paper plans into a living television programme. No matter what the number of sources, live, recorded, visual, oral, static, moving, they have to knit the whole structure together into one piece, each dove-tailing neatly into the next to produce a continuous, seamless whole based on split-second timing.

That is not over-stating the case. Split seconds make all the difference between a programme which flows from item to item without a hiccup and one which is ragged, with awkward delays between newsreader introduction and film, clipped sound, momentarily blank screen and missed cues. Yet there is a very fine margin indeed between success and failure. The most ambitious programmes, especially, court disaster night after night, pushing men, women and machinery to the limits by the deliberate policy of trying to squeeze in the very latest information. New stories are added, some dropped, others altered right up to and including the time the programme is on the air; the only dead-line most

172

editors are prepared to accept is the end of the programme.

As a result, the professionalism and expertise of the gallery staff is continuously on trial. One slip, and all the time, effort and money spent by others might be wasted. Fortunately, real disasters are fairly rare, despite the knowledge that one minor misfortune has a habit of begetting another, and the prickly feeling that, one day, an entire programme is going to collapse like a house of cards.

The captain of the ship during the voyage of transmission is the *studio director* (*production assistant* or *PA*). Much depends on his reflexes, not only in times of crisis, but also in the execution of the run-of-the-mill programmes which seem to be sailing along without trouble. It helps if the PA does not go 'cold' into the gallery. Indeed, some organisations may insist that he is always on hand to act as a link between editorial and production staff. To do that effectively he needs to sit in on the conferences at which the running orders are drawn up, ready to sound the warning bells over any potential difficulty. Then, once the conference is over, the PA is expected to keep in close touch with the newsroom so that there is a minimum of delay in passing on alterations to the running order.

Another of the PA's most important functions takes place well before transmission. This is a discussion with the film editing department about *film make-up*—the physical joining of a programme's separate films into their proper order for transmission. Make-up, though not a particularly arduous task for the film editor concerned, needs care and a certain amount of time. As one film is joined to the next it is wound on to a spool down as far as the twenty-fifth frame from the end. At this point a circular-shaped mark known as a *cue-dot* is scratched on to the surface, in the top right hand corner of the frame. This gives the production team in the gallery a crucial one-second warning that the film is about to finish, in effect telling them to prepare the next source. Sepmag sound tracks are joined together on another reel, exactly in parallel so that there is no loss of synchronism with the picture during transmission.

Where more than one telecine machine is available, the PA usually asks for the films to be shared between them. This has a number of advantages. Spreading the load obviously reduces the likelihood of total chaos in the event of one telecine machine breaking down. It also gives editors the freedom to 'drop' films, even on the air, for space reasons. The unwanted film is simply run

THE CONTROL ROOM—A TYPICAL LAYOUT

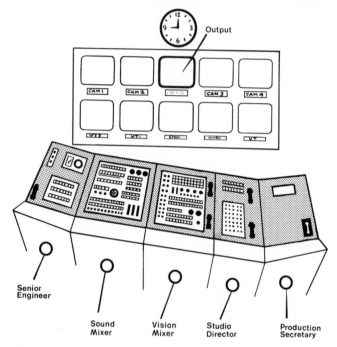

Output

Senior Engineer

Sound Mixer

Vision Mixer

Studio Director

Production Secretary

Fig. 38. The bank of monitors above the desk gives the studio director a chance to preview the picture available from each source before selecting it.

through, unseen by the viewing audience, at a time when another reel is in use.

Although gallery layouts vary, a typical one (Fig. 38) has the PA seated at a wide desk which runs virtually the whole width of the room facing the bank of monitors. Immediately on his right sits the *production secretary*, armed with stop-watches to see that the whole programme runs exactly to time, and that an accurate count-down is given into and out of the separate film, videotape and other inserts as the broadcast proceeds. On the left of the director is the *vision mixer*, the buttons and levers built into an organ keyboard above the desk top, allowing him to select sources as directed. Next to the vision mixer is either the *sound mixer*, busy at a panel of faders, or a *senior engineer*, whose prime responsibility is to ensure that technical standards are maintained throughout the broadcast.

This, then, would be the basic gallery crew, although there

might be a second sound mixer and the operators for the sophisticated remotely-controlled cameras favoured by some news services (see below). Some organisations make do without the engineer's presence in the gallery, locating him and his equipment in another technical area. Others expect the director to double as vision mixer by punching his own buttons.

Other places in the gallery may be found for the senior editorial staff responsible for the programme, and representatives of other departments who have made special contributions, an assistant from stills and the film editor responsible for make-up. With all these experts on the spot, answers to any problem which may crop up during transmission can be supplied very quickly.

In the studio

Unless it is autonomous or just plain lucky, the news is likely to be only one of a number of programme types queueing up to take turns in using whatever studio facilities its parent organisation has to offer. Big television productions need plenty of space and technical support; studios exclusively for news tend to be small and unelaborate. After all, very little of a half hour news programme is spent *in* the studio compared with the time devoted to routing videotape, film, and other sources *through* it.

Even so, as it is largely on studio-based items that programme identity is maintained, considerable thought has to go into their technical presentation. To do that there might be up to four television cameras. One concentrates on a head and shoulders of the newsreader, two on stills and maps, and a fourth is reserved for additional performers (reporters and correspondents) or the occasional interviewee. Movements are so few and unfussy that the BBC, for example, has found it just as effective to use colour cameras remotely controlled by operators sitting not in the studio but at a bank of switches in the control gallery several feet away. Each camera is equipped with an electronic 'memory' capable of storing up to twenty pre-selected shots for use on transmission, thus removing much of the mental strain from the camerawork needed for a very quickly moving programme.

Studio sound is fed in independently from microphones sited in pairs (in case one fails) at each of the reading positions. Overhead, individually adjustable banks of lights hang down from hoists close to the ceiling, throwing their beams over studio sets intended to convey the atmosphere of the programme.

Some sets are elaborate and expensive affairs. One American station is reputed to have spent three hundred thousand dollars on the design for a daily *local* programme. Much favoured are desks on raised platforms, surrounded by simulated book-shelves or 'windows' which allow the viewer to look out on familiar 'views', photographically reproduced. Other sets are of stark simplicity, consisting of plain backgrounds against which the newsreader sits at an ordinary desk equipped with only the bare essentials of telephone (to talk to the director in emergencies), microphone and cue lights.

For some years past it has been fashionable to present the reader against a background changing to give visual representation of each item being read. This might be a map, still, or some kind of symbol. The refinement has been possible since the days before colour television, and is still used in countries where the change from black and white has not yet taken place.

Two basic systems are in use, the most effective being *back projection* (*BP*), which is cheap to install and simple to operate. A slide projector, usually 35 mm, is placed on the studio floor some distance behind the reader and is adjusted to throw its image on to a translucent screen. Reader and picture are in turn photographed together from the front by the studio camera, the effect on the viewer being to make it seem as though the reader and background are complementary. It is possible to change backgrounds in front of the viewer's eyes by using a second projector and operating the two alternately. A reasonably large studio is needed so that the space between projector and screen is sufficient to create a picture which fills the screen. Also, the BP operator has to remember to reverse the slides when loading them into the projector so that they appear to be the correct way round when viewed from the front.

The second system is *front projection*. This is very similar to BP, except that the image is projected from the front, as its name suggests. It is more likely to be used where studio space is limited, and can be most effective provided that care is taken with lighting to see that no shadows appear on the screen behind the reader.

The whole idea of background systems has been revolutionised with the coming of colour television and the invention of *colour separation overlay* (*CSO*). This highly sophisticated device enables a plain background to be replaced electronically by another visual ingredient without affecting the subject in the fore-ground.

176

The key to the CSO system lies in the colour chosen for the studio backcloth. It is often blue, of which there is very little in human flesh tones. At the touch of a switch, the electronic camera locks on to that background colour, filling it with a picture coming from another source—perhaps a second camera, a caption scanner or a videotape recorder—effectively merging the two images into one. What is created for the viewer is a kind of optical illusion; should the newsreader look over his shoulder he would see nothing but the plain backcloth.

Such flaws as exist in the system seem to be only minor. Occasionally, when blue is used, a foreground subject will take on a blue-tinged outline round the hair, and a zooming-in movement of the camera seems to make the foreground leap forward by itself. CSO is activated by any strong foreground colour which matches the background, so clothing should be selected with care, otherwise the unfortunate performer will have to suffer the embarrassment of being told that the background picture can be seen through an electronic 'hole' punched in his or her body.

CSO development is by no means complete and it seems quite possible that, in the future, sets will be almost entirely replaced by *electronic* versions created out of colour transparencies.

Other floor space in the studio is taken up by coils of camera cable, large pin-boards or stands to accommodate stills and maps, and portable monitor sets which enable the reader to keep a discreet check both on the output and his own performance. Tucked away in the studio corners are the controls for the script-reading devices, together with one or two operators, and a small table at which the writers sit to operate the cue lights on the reader's desk during voice-over commentaries (see page 178).

During transmission the floor manager stays in the studio as a go-between for the director in the gallery and the performers at their desks, making sure that any late instructions or alterations are passed on, helping to count readers in and out of the various sequences, and giving whatever visual cues may be necessary.

In recent years some of the floor manager's task has been lightened by the introduction of *deaf-aids*, miniature loudspeakers tailored to fit snugly into the ear of each regular performer. These are linked directly with the director's microphone in the gallery, but some readers prefer to switch them off for long periods during transmission in case peripheral babble by production staff breaks through to distract them.

Count-down to transmission

An hour or so before transmission (the precise timing depends on the duration and complexity of each programme) the production staff gather in the control gallery for the *script conference*. At this stage in the proceedings the PA has the running order, at least some of the alterations which have inevitably been made, and a good idea of what else may change before the programme goes out on the air. Now he is able to begin issuing detailed instructions, referring to the items on the running order in sequence, page by page.

Everyone involved is made familiar with the make-up of the telecine reels, the machine-by-machine allocation of videotaped items, and given an idea of the order of graphics and stills. Instructions are marked on whatever pages of the script have been distributed up to that time. For those still to come the instructions are written on a *skeleton*, a sheet which is left completely blank apart from the corresponding page number of the script. When the script page eventually turns up, the skeleton will be thrown away, although in fact the director *could* work from the blank page as a last resort.

This is how the dialogue might go for part of a script conference for The Five O'Clock Report:

> (PA speaking) ". . . so it's page ten next—strike. That'll be camera one for the reader, into library film—the first on reel two. OK? They've written in a page twelve for the industrial correspondent's studio spot, though it might not happen. If it does, we'll sit him on camera four with a CSO of the factory using a slide from scanner one. I suppose they'll want to superimpose his name and title as well. That'll be on scanner two. Right, then it's back to Phil and Camera one for page thirteen, the pay off. No page fourteen, so page fifteen is next, factory fire. Camera one for Phil, plus a map. That better be pinned up for Camera two, I think, because the writer wants us to zoom in on the street name. We'll rehearse that later if we can. From there it's VT two with fire midlands. That's going to be so late there's a chance that it'll have to be live . . ."

The conference continues briskly in the same vein, with pauses for the director to answer queries from other members of the production staff. Eventually every page on the running order has been covered, and allowance made for those items about which

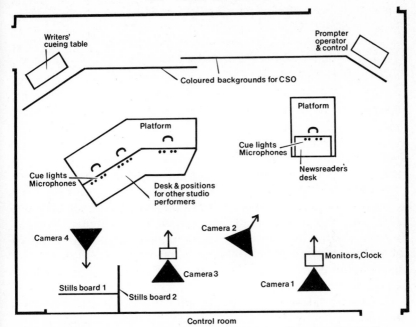

Fig. 39. Possible four-camera layout for a news studio. Camera 3, when not in use, covers stills board 2; cameras 2 and 4 can be moved to cover the other contributors at the big desk.

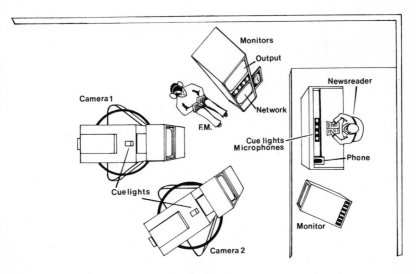

Fig. 40. The studio, as seen from the newsreader's desk.

very little is so far known. Everybody concerned with the production is now fully aware of the part he is expected to play, while being quite prepared to accommodate any sudden change of plan. It is a fairly routine day for news, however, and with the favoured editorial shift on duty, the production staff are keeping their fingers crossed for an easy ride.

Rehearsal

Rehearsals for television news programmes tend to be sketchy affairs for the reason that so much of the material to be used on transmission is unavailable until the last few minutes before airtime. Scripts are still being written, films edited, recordings made.

Nevertheless, the director must go through whatever he can. An early, completed reel gives him the chance to check at least some of the film, to try out the zoom in to the map on page fifteen, and see whether the script for the end item on page fifty-seven of the running order will fit by giving the reader a canter through it. As the minutes tick away, the flow of completed scripts coming into the control gallery begins to quicken. The corresponding skeletons are thrown out to accommodate the new pages, everybody remembering to transfer the marks made so carefully at the script conference forty minutes earlier. Sometimes there are variations:

> PA: Page thirty eight, everyone. There's an extra still. Camera three, all right?

Sometimes there are deletions ordered by the editor speaking on the intercom from the newsroom:

> PA: Page forty four, Missing Paintings, is out. That means we shan't want your Goya portrait, Scanner two, thank you.

In between, the industrial correspondent wanders into the studio, and is motioned into a seat facing camera four. The floor manager's voice booms into the gallery from next door:

> FM: Can you try the voice level for Michael now, please? He's got to go back into the newsroom to check on his story.
> PA: Yes, right away. Sound? (He presses a button which allows the correspondent in the studio to hear him.) Just a few words then, Michael. (After no more than

a sentence the sound mixer in the gallery has adjusted the fader and given the thumbs up.) OK, thanks. (To production secretary): Better get the make-up girl in here. He'll need a touch of powder before he goes on.

With ten minutes to go, the editor in the newsroom is suddenly faced with the sort of dilemma he has nightmares about. The reporter in charge of the factory fire story in the midlands has telephoned to say that a search of the gutted building revealed another three bodies, bringing the known death toll to five. What is more, police have told him that ten more workers are unaccounted for, although it is not yet apparent whether they had reported for duty that day, and the checking procedure is a slow one.

The editor curses the timidity which led him to regard the economics story as the most important, inconclusive though it was. The fire now has all the makings of a major disaster. There is still time to switch the lead, but it would mean wholesale changes to the running order and destroying much of the carefully-planned structure of the programme. And that is taking no account of the risks involved in such an upheaval, so late. Fortunately, this PA is up to it. With others, perhaps . . . One more question remains to be answered:

Editor: What's happening about the strike? Are they going to settle?

Writer: Michael's on the phone now—it doesn't look as though the meeting has finished yet.

The editor makes up his mind:

Editor: (To his No. 2). Right. I'm going to switch the lead.

We'll move the fire up to page two, with vision, map and VT. And we'll put the collision at page three— vision, map and film. That means fifteen, sixteen, eighteen and nineteen are out. You tell the gallery; I'm on my way there now. And get the headlines re-written.

In the semi-darkness a few yards down the corridor, the PA is still in the process of catching up with earlier changes:

PA: There's a new story at page thirty five, Commons

Debate. Camera one for the reader and a still of Frank Smith on camera three. And pages fifty six and fifty seven are out. Out. That means we don't need your last film, Weigh-in Today, on Reel Three, thank you. (To floor manager): Tell Phil we now go straight from the Marathon Man VT on page fifty four to the close, OK? Right, script check in five minutes everybody.

By now the messengers are bustling in with the last scripts. Everybody is writing furiously. The floor is littered with discarded skeletons and 'dropped' story scripts. In the studio the make-up girl is applying a light touch of powder to the industrial correspondent's forehead. The newsreader is checking the roll of Autocue against the duplicated pages of script.

The editor has arrived in the gallery and has begun to explain the late changes. The PA is unperturbed. He speaks calmly into the microphone linking him with the studio and the other technical areas:

PA: Change of lead coming up. I'll tell you in a moment, during the script check.

The last changes are scribbled in on the running order. The editor, with time to look round for a few moments, indicates the preview monitor for camera three, which is just lining up on its still for the late story:

Editor: Is that the Frank Smith still? I thought he'd shaved off his beard.

The stills assistant hurries out to check with the writer back in the newsroom.

Five minutes to go. 'Script check,' orders the PA. This is the last check before transmission, and everyone is expected to pay full attention. Loss of concentration here could result in disaster later on. Again, the PA is in command, going through the complete script, page by page, at a rapid pace, in confirmation of all that has gone on before and since the script conference nearly an hour before.

PA: Here we go then. We start with the 'Five O'Clock Report' caption on scanner one, with the signature tune on quarter-inch tape. Then there's a re-write of page one, menu, on its way. That's Phil's voice over camera two still, scanner one still, back to camera two, then

182

scanner one again. The new lead is numbered page two, factory fire. Phil on camera one, the map we rehearsed on camera two. That's a quick change for you, two, remember. Then VT-one for the fire/midlands report— *was* numbered page sixteen. Explain when I get there. Page three is now ship collision. Camera one, map on scanner two, film on reel three. Then page four, Prime Minister. Camera one, film interview on reel one, camera one again for the reaction, plus stills on camera two and scanner one. Page seven, PM/Political is the live inject. He'll end by handing back to the studio . . .

The PA rattles through it all, remembering to explain how pages two and three have taken the places of fifteen, sixteen, eighteen and nineteen. The few queries take only seconds to answer. "Two minutes to go," calls the production secretary. Red flashing lights outside the studio and gallery doors warn that transmission is imminent.

The studio begins to settle down. The Autocue operator is back at the controls of her machine. The newsreader takes a last brief look at the knot in his tie as reflected in one of the monitors. Music filters into the studio, signifying the approaching end of the preceding programme.

One minute. A writer races into the studio with the rewritten headline page. In the back of the gallery a fierce argument is going on between another writer and the stills assistant about the Frank Smith portrait. Voices rise several decibels.

Thirty seconds. The PA reluctantly turns his attention from the monitor bank:

> PA: Quiet, please! Stand by everyone. Stand by scanner one with the titles and stand by quarter-inch tape.

Station announcements are coming to an end in the brief break between programmes. A square cue dot appears in the top left-hand corner of the monitor which is now showing station identification and a clock.

Fifteen seconds. The dot disappears. Ten seconds. Nine. Eight. Seven. Continuity announcer: . . . that's at eight-thirty. But now, at Five O'Clock, it's time for the news.

> PA: Cut to Scanner one with the opening titles. Go tape. Coming to studio and camera two. (The signature tune ends) Cue him . . . and cut to two!

Reader: At least five people have died in a big factory fire in the midlands; the number *could* go as high as fifteen. In the Channel . . .

PA: Scanner one next. Cut!

Reader: The Prime Minister says . . .

Production Secretary: Thirty seconds, VT-one. (There is an answering buzz from the machine operator on the floor below. The PA, following the script, waits until the reader gets to within exactly thirty three words before the end of the introduction.)

PA: (crisply) Run VT-one.

Production Secretary: Nine, eight, seven.

Reader: . . . just received this report from Tom Dixon.

Production Secretary: . . . three, two, one, zero.

PA: Cut to VT. (He relaxes) A little more headroom on your newsreader shot, please camera one. He's looking a bit squashed. Where the hell has Michael gone?

Floor Manager: He's just gone back to the newsroom to make a check call.

PA: (grumpily) What am I to do if he doesn't make it? Show an empty chair? We've got about three and a half minutes before we come to him. (Wearily) Will they never learn?

Editor: (reassuringly) He'll be back.

Production Secretary: Thirty seconds to go on this VT.

PA: OK. Stand by telecine reel one, please. Coming to camera one next. That's much better, thanks, one. (To the Editor) Are you happy about the Smith still yet?

Editor: We're working on it.

Production	
Secretary:	Ten to go.
PA:	And where's bloody Michael? Coming to camera one . . .
Production	
Secretary:	. . . three, two, one . . .
PA:	Cue him and cut!

Hardened newspeople still manage to marvel at the way in which the production staff throw an almost entirely unrehearsed programme on the air without so much as the hint of a hitch. The occasions when minor errors occur, the PA running the film too early or too late, the vision mixer pressing the wrong button, the scanner operator getting the stills out of order, are usually the subject of heated inquest. Audiences probably do not notice unless the mistakes are glaring, and then they seem to take huge delight in discovering that their favourite news programme is peopled by fallible human beings just like themselves, and not robots.

Most of the mistakes which *are* made could be avoided, but that would mean setting strict deadlines to ensure full rehearsals. It is not a realistic proposition. Television newspeople are acutely conscious of the 'now or never' aspect of their work. That is why editors are prepared to jeopardise their entire production for the sake of a good story breaking ten minutes into the programme. By dropping one vision item, taking the option of an 'early out' on a videotape insert and striking out all but one of the closing headlines, there is suddenly enough room to squeeze in something which may already be too late for some editions of tomorrow's morning newspapers. And that, television journalists will say with satisfaction, is what it's all about.

News magazine format

What has gone before has been principally to do with programmes which bring news to national audiences. But these, despite the enormous followings they command, are easily outstripped in numbers and popularity by those concentrating on local matters— news magazines which have hard news sheltering under the same roof as interviews and longer film reports categorised as 'news features' or 'current affairs'.

At their best, these programmes are more accurate mirrors of society than their national counterparts can ever hope to be, and local politicians anxious to keep a finger on the public pulse often consider them required viewing. Content is a broad mixture of the serious and the frivolous, the contentious issues either purely local or national ones given a local twist. On the 'magazine' side, daily film reports and studio discussions presided over by the main anchormen are supplemented by regular feature items which might include viewers' letters, consumer affairs, theatre, cinema and press reviews. The 'news', sometimes read by a separate presenter, comes in the shape of mini bulletins containing stills, graphics and mostly mute film.

The pace in a local newsroom is bound to be more leisurely and some of the issues less immediate, but for the aspiring television journalist, work on a news magazine may be far more stimulating than that on a nationally-based programme. Staffs are invariably smaller and harder-pressed, opening the way for those with ambition to learn their way about very quickly and to turn their hand to many different tasks. As a result, a surprising number who start out as local newswriters soon find themselves taking to the road as reporters, ultimately perhaps, at national level.

There is also something immensely satisfying about being so close to the grass roots. Many of the subjects handled by national programme newswriters cannot be anything except remote from the vast audiences of millions. Local television journalists live with the knowledge that what they write about directly touches the lives of their viewers. It helps to make them more careful. Instead of writing rude letters, complaining members of the public are liable to come round to the office and hammer on the door for an answer face-to-face or accost any programme 'personalities' they are likely to spot shopping in the supermarket with their families in tow.

Journalistic frustrations come later. Money and technical resources may be limited, the same events come along with boring regularity year after year, and when an exceptional local event does take on wider significance the national news bosses are probably waiting in the wings, ready to skim off all the cream. The fact that one of the prime functions of a local newsroom might be to supply the network with coverage does not make the divided responsibility any easier to bear. The satisfaction of contributing to a national programme is inevitably tempered by the knowledge that an item so used is then either 'lost' for local consumption, or must be re-shaped somehow before being shown again to viewers who have already seen most of it on the network.

Complacency creeps in, manifesting itself in a cosy relationship with regular viewers in a way which seems deliberately designed to exclude outsiders. I once spent the best part of a month watching an otherwise excellent daily local programme which made the irritating assumption that every member of the audience knew each exact location mentioned. It was always plain 'Smith Road', and never 'Smith Road, south Blankville', and I pitied anyone genuinely needing to know the geography.

By far the biggest headache for the editor of a local programme is how to fill the allotted twenty five, thirty or forty minutes every weekday tea-time. The staff may not be large enough to allow for a continuously high level of sophisticated planning, so much of each programme may have to be assembled from scratch, a matter of hours before the day's transmission.

That leaves little room for manoeuvre, and should the already meagre ration of stories be reduced for some reason, the alternative to the unthinkable, leaving a hole, is to pad out what is left. The result is not attractive. The live studio interview may have to be stretched to an extra minute even though the subject has been exhausted long before. The film editor may be called on to rummage among the trims for extra shots he would prefer to discard. The 'news' slot may be crammed with another handful of vision stories which really deserve to be spiked. So, instead of being a brief, crisply-written round up of matters of real local interest, the news becomes a convenient kind of dustbin for dumping trivialities unwanted anywhere else.

Before long, if these conditions persist, standards slip, fundamentals like shot-listing are ignored, and the whole programme becomes flabby and over-written. The journalist's ancient battle-cry of "What's it worth?" is replaced by the anxious inquiry: "How long can you make it?" This is an understandable attitude, but one which does disservice to the viewer. Almost every story has its own 'natural' length, in whatever context it may be found. Going beyond it does nothing except debase the coinage.

That, admittedly, begs the question of how else a programme is to be filled. Frankly there is no answer beyond the general argument which says that by some means or other, more effort must be put into the organisation of newsgathering, even at the expense of temporarily weakening output.

Newsreader or newscaster?

It was President Harry Truman who immortalised the saying "The buck stops here". Conceivably, in his case, it was true. The widespread misconception about 'The Buck' in television news is that *it* stops at the desk of the person seen to be responsible for delivering the message, good or bad, directly to the viewer. In other words, the newsreader.

When a new editor took over BBC news, "some critics complained of the space that newspapers gave to the story, the way they treated Angela Rippon (one of the newsreaders) as though she had won an Oscar. These critics were wrong. The men and women who read the news play a large, persistent and recurring part in the people's lives."[1]

Newsreaders themselves have been known to compare their role with the town criers of old, the main difference being that the word is passed on to the people from a comfortable seat in a television studio rather than from among jostling crowds in the market-square. And on a much, much more personal level:

> "Television breeds a closeness and intimacy quite unlike that of any other medium," says Robert Dougall, who read the news on BBC television for more than fifteen years. "Your image is projected straight into people's homes. You become, as it were, a privileged guest at innumerable firesides. What is more, a newsreader is not playing a role, not appearing as another character, or in costume, but as himself. He therefore builds up over the years a kind of rapport with the public."[2]

The responsibility all that implies is fairly awesome. There is still more. A cough, hesitation or mispronunciation might easily make nonsense of the most serious or important piece of news. An erratic or unpredictable speed of delivery, particularly during the crucial few seconds of countdown into film or videotaped inserts, can have a devastatingly destructive effect on the most carefully planned programme.

Yet ever since the far-off days when he was expected to present the news anonymously out of vision (in case an accidentally raised eyebrow, twitch, or some other inadvertent facial expression should be construed by the viewer as 'comment') the con-

---

[1] Jeremy Bugler, *The Listener*, April 1, 1976.
[2] Robert Dougall, *In and Out of the Box*. (Collins/Harvill 1973.)

ventional newsreader has always been a rather contradictory figure. On the one hand he is accepted as the figurehead, the standard-bearer of the programme, admired, respected, the subject of unwavering public interest on and off the screen. On the other, he is among the last people to be consulted about content, style and format. Complaints that newsreader A makes certain grammatical errors that newsreader B scrupulously avoids overlook the fact that neither has probably very much to do with the way the words are written, only the way they are read.

So, sitting in front of a camera, reading aloud the fruits of other people's labour with the aid of a written script and prompter device, directed through a hidden ear-piece by a production assistant next door, chaperoned by the floor manager standing no more than a few feet away, supplied with a card index or other reference system to help with pronunciation, the newsreader has a task which, on the surface at any rate, scarcely seems exacting enough to warrant all that public acclaim. No job for a man, as one reader himself has wryly described it. True, there are nightly butterflies to be conquered for those terrified of making a mistake or losing the place on the page in front of millions; and yes, the hot lights may make the half hour or so of transmission a trifle uncomfortable physically, especially if fairly formal dress is required on the set. But even here the standard 'newsreader shot' usually reveals no more than the upper half of the body. The rest might just as well be covered by crumpled old jeans or a pair of shorts, for all the viewer knows. Before Angela Rippon danced in a BBC Christmas show, critics of news programmes had indeed been known to inquire, rather cruelly, whether newsreaders needed legs at all.

As for the qualifications necessary for the work, these would seem to be limited to an authoritative screen 'presence', a pleasant appearance, clear diction, lack of irritating mannerisms and an ability to keep cool when things occasionally fall apart at the seams —talents which, it may be said, bear an uncanny resemblance to those required for ordinary television reporting.

Here is another contradiction: not every newsreader is a reporter who has come in from the cold. Readers of the news are not necessarily fully-fledged journalists at all, although they seem bound to admit that they could scarcely be effective unless they were deeply interested in the subject. Some began as actors, announcers for different kinds of programmes, or were chosen simply because they had the looks and voices to suit the times.

Some people in television are convinced that the days of the non-journalist newsreader are strictly limited, the end being hastened by technical advances, notably in ENG, where the transmission of live pictures through the studio demands immediate *journalistic* interpretation. Some would say that the movement began long ago, pointing to the introduction of *newscasters*, allegedly a very different breed of animal altogether. The newscaster, goes the theory, is employed to fulfil the same functions as the old-fashioned newsreader, except that he is also expected to make positive contributions to a programme from a position of considerable journalistic experience (drawn from inside or outside television) either by writing some of it, acting as an interviewer within it, or both. As the price for such professional expertise, programme bosses are prepared to accept less than cut-glass accents and features which, in the case of one much-loved veteran performer, I have heard described politely as 'lived in'.

However, on a practical level, such is the complexity of television news, with its last minute film and videotaped items, Eurovision or satellite contributions, it is arguable whether anyone less than a superhuman figure is able to do very much more than ask the questions as suggested to them by producers or researchers, or tinker with a few of the news scripts in order to suit a personal style.

That knowledge has not prevented a further development, in some quarters, of the 'personalised' news, which deliberately sets out to identify one individual reader so closely with a particular programme that his or her name is even included as part of the title.

The idea, presumably, is to encourage the audience to establish much the same kind of special, trusting relationship with the person bringing them their daily dose of news as they have with their doctors, bank managers and similar professional advisers. The expectation seems to be that the personality reader has a greater chance of building up a devoted following sufficient to resist any opposition from other channels than the man or woman who appears on the conventional news programme in rotation as part of a reading team.

At this point, I must admit to prejudice. From a working journalist's point of view it seems entirely wrong to sacrifice the broad team concept in favour of one dominant presenter figure, who might possibly become what one television news editor has

190

bluntly described as 'an uncontrollable monster', and probably a very expensive one at that.

It is also the very antithesis of the idea of the television news-reader as a dispassionate provider of information, the programme becoming instead a vehicle for one person's interpretation of events for the viewer to swallow undiluted or turn off. The other question to be asked is what happens when the 'oracle' is temporarily absent, leaves or dies? The answer is that a vacuum is left, the programme becomes rudderless until he returns, an acceptable substitute is found, or the entire format is changed.

Perhaps the last words on the subject are best left to an outsider. Alan Coren, a humorous, often very accurate observer of the British television scene, in examining ITN's search for a female newscaster to rival the astonishing popularity of the BBC's Angela Rippon (". . . from the status of mere face to that of international phenomenon . . ."), perceived some disturbing auguries for responsible television newscasting:

> ". . . news is, quite simply, something that happens while you're not there. You therefore require to be informed of it in as clear, cool, detailed, objective and interesting a way as possible; news is not entertainment. When the priorities in its presentation shift so that the criteria become glamour, personality and mass-audience appeal, news is no longer news but feature journalism."[1]

Doing it in pairs

A popular alternative to the solo newsreader supported by the occasional reporter or specialist correspondent presenting individual items in the studio is the newsreading double-act, personified by the highly-successful Huntley-Brinkley partnership on American television.

It is a good idea, particularly when used as a means of giving a facelift to a tired presentation, but it is not as easy to put into practice as might be supposed. The introduction of a second person into a formerly single-reader news set-up adds technical complications, possibly leading to a complete redesign of the studio to make room for another camera. More thought has to be given to backings and lighting so that there is continuity when the two newsreaders are shown separately in successive one-shots. Where other contributors are also expected to appear regularly,

---

[1] *London Evening Standard*, April 4, 1977.

there is also the danger that the programme will seem to be cluttered with too many faces barring the way between the viewer and the news.

Next, it presumes the discovery of not one but *two* first-class readers willing to pool their talents for the sake of the common good. Compatibility is essential; the whole enterprise is as good as doomed if (as has been known) one of the more established readers is reluctant to share the studio with anyone else, regarding the new partner as an unworthy intruder.

Although the camera may show them together in the same shot for only a few seconds at either end of the programme possibly half an hour apart, the best pairs are able to give the impression that, however much their individual styles differ, they hit it off as a team, each member of it taking a genuine, continuing interest in what the other is doing, and not acting as one of two people who just happen to find themselves occupying the same set at the same time. These experts somehow manage to 'bounce' off one another, each using perhaps no more than a hint of a head turn away from the partner's direction before taking up a new story. Their manner is crisp, efficient and friendly, without recourse to the cosy, ultra-informality which looks and sounds so phoney.

Long discussions go on about how the work should be split between two newsreaders. What was special about Huntley-Brinkley was that one was in Washington and the other in New York, which resulted in a fairly natural division of responsibility. Other pairs have been known to split home and foreign stories, to take alternative whole items, or what amount to alternate pages of script. Sequences of out of vision commentaries when spoken by alternate readers come across with real pace and punch, particularly when the partnership consists of one female and one male.

Working with the newsreader

Other members of the news team are likely to regard their news reading colleagues, whether one or two, with considerable professional respect as the instrument by which a series of previously unrelated events becomes a television programme before their eyes. They know that, without the reader, that transformation would not be possible. Those programmes which have a succession of reporters popping up in the studio to introduce their own items are deluding themselves if they believe they have done something different. All they have done is to share out one role between many, for the function of linking one news event to the next remains the same whoever does it.

A few of the staff, perhaps other journalists among them, may have a tendency to feel resentful about the way that such an apparently undemanding job as reading the news generally rates super-star treatment. Short of suggesting that they try it for themselves, the only sensible advice to give them is to stop worrying and start appreciating how their work benefits from having it well presented. For while a poor newsreader can certainly ruin a good script, the corollary of that is that a good newsreader can improve on a poor one.

The 'writer's reader' has many qualities, mostly invisible to anyone except the insider. These include a natural gift for putting the emphasis in the right place, even on late scripts which have to be sight-read for the first time on transmission, the occasional offer of exactly the right word or phrase which might have eluded the hard-pressed writer for hours, razor-sharp reactions to cues from the floor or the gallery and the confidence and ability to smooth over the awkward moments which might otherwise lead to disaster.

At the other extreme is the reader who is over-anxious, egotistical and temperamental, unwilling to accept advice, concerned only that the duties he is called upon to perform do not offend his public image, uncaring about the hair-raising rides he gives production and editorial staff on transmission by speeding up or slowing down delivery as the mood takes him.

Not all programmes employ their newsreaders full-time, effectively ruling out close collaboration with editorial staff, but where possible readers should always be invited to attend conferences in order to absorb the feel of a day's news before they might have to read it.

As transmission time approaches, readers should be warned of running order changes, awkward or unusual words. Any last-minute alterations to completed scripts must also be given (if necessary, in a suitable lull during transmission) to the prompter operators when they affect vision passages. Where necessary, writers should be prepared to alter words and phrases to suit the reader's style, so long as the intended sense is not destroyed. Much, of course, depends on the writer's skill in constructing the short, easy-to-understand, easy-to-read sentences already discussed. Tongue-twisters of the "Scottish soldier shot in the shoulder" variety are easily avoided if the writer reads scripts to himself before inflicting them on the poor newsreader.

Some problem words, however, are unavoidable. One world-famous newsreader, otherwise impeccable in his delivery, admits to great difficulty in saying 'hostage', a word much in current use, alas, and one for which there are not many obvious alternatives. Pity more the former newsreader who was virtually incapable of pronouncing an almost endless list of words which writers went through incredible verbal contortions to avoid using. Eventually, after much suffering, one hit on the bright idea of spelling out the 'difficult' words phonetically on the scripts. "Why not?" replied the exasperated editor for the day, "We've tried everything else except injections".

CONCLUSION

THE whole emphasis of this book has deliberately been on method, not motive. *Why* individual television news services choose to operate the way they do, especially in the hyper-sensitive area of news selection is a matter between them and their public. Each is guided by its own set of principles, most of which have their origins in the political and social ethos of the country in which they are broadcasting. And, since increasingly large numbers of broadcasting organisations are owned by govern-ments, it follows that what passes for news in one country will not necessarily match the concept of what passes for news in another. For every journalist struggling towards the goal of 'balanced objectivity' there are others for whom such niceties are of no concern. By choice or by compulsion, their roles are seen in an entirely different light. To put it another way, one man's objective report revealing government incompetence is another's betrayal of the society which succours him.

One experienced journalist, seconded as news adviser to the television station of a Middle Eastern kingdom, was quite unable to persuade those in charge that their news judgement was at fault because they insisted on beginning every programme with the filmed official activities of the king, followed by the filmed official activities of the queen then the crown prince, and so on right the way through the royal household, at diminishing duration and in order of importance. All this was followed by speeches by the prime minister and the activities of other govern-ment ministers. Afterwards came domestic news, most of it of stunning triviality. Then, and only then, about half way through the programme, was space given to what the adviser recognised as 'real' news, regardless of its importance. The fact that while he was there Neil Armstrong was taking man's first step on the moon, made no difference to the rigid pattern.

195

Later during the adviser's stay a revolution took place. The monarchy was overthrown and exiled, and a republic proclaimed. The editors of the news responded at once. From then on, every programme began with the filmed official activities of the president of the revolutionary council, then the filmed official activities of each council member in turn. Domestic news came next, followed by the foreign news, in much the same way as before. The royal family was totally ignored. Those working on the programme made no protest. They merely carried on doing what they saw as their duty as journalists, serving the interests of the state. The fact that the circumstances had changed drastically made no difference to their attitude.

That approach commands widespread support. Waclaw Wyglecdowski, head of the Intervision News Exchange of OIRT (the East European equivalent of Eurovision) describes television news in the socialist countries as "politically involved information services".[1] The foremost aim is the "reliable presentation of news items dealing with topical events and exerting a definite influence upon public opinion. Therefore they do not seek sensation; crimes, disasters, accidents and scandals do not predominate. Such events cannot push aside news items of interest to the majority of viewers. The presentation of acts of violence is very limited."

On the other hand, television news broadcasts "do try to portray social processes and the development of the socialist society. The processes of socialist integration constitute a major subject of reporting, too. Moreover events reflecting the fight and struggle for freedom, peace and social progress all over the world are themes occurring very often."

Editors are well aware that their output is a public commentary. "They know that it is impossible to present news broadcasts without influencing the audience . . . often the mere inclusion of a particular item in the news service, *or its omission* (italics added), already constitutes a commentary."

To Western viewers, such television news would come under the category of propaganda, and probably dull propaganda at that. Just as one British television journalist, after a visit to China, described how he could not get used to the idea of watching the main news programme on Peking television end with brief sequences or headlines of the news to be seen the *next* night.

But how much worse is that than the example of the long-

---

[1] *EBU Review*, May, 1975.

defunct American television news programme whose cigarette company sponsors forbade the inclusion of any shots of 'No Smoking' signs and allowed only Winston Churchill to be seen smoking a cigar? Or 'McLurg's Law' (so named after a senior television news editor) which says that the death of, or injury to one person from your own country is, in terms of news value, equal to the deaths of or injuries to very much larger, unspecified, numbers of foreigners, depending on how far away they live?

Pierre Brunel-Lantenac, Head of the EBU Television News and Special Operations Service, puts much the same thing rather more eloquently: "Television is subject to the tyranny of the stopwatch. In twenty or twenty five minutes of pictures and commentary we have to show the essential facts in the awareness that such is man's nature that a trivial incident occurring on his own doorstep sometimes involves him more deeply than an event of fundamental human significance on the other side of the globe that, without his realising it, will affect the future of mankind."[1]

Robin Day believes that the selection of news items for British television is often dictated not by importance but by the availability of visually exciting film. "The news values of television, transmitted into every home every night, must be sober, balanced and responsible. If they continually overemphasise the violent, the sensational and the trivial, whether for pictorial reasons or because of an urge to be parochial or 'popular', television will be a corrupting and degrading influence on all our thoughts and attitudes . . . No one has any right to assume that the values of television news today will not exert a powerful influence on the values of society tomorrow."[2]

The arguments have been raging since television news began to matter. No doubt they will continue as long as it exists in its present form. For the reporters, writers, film editors and directors trapped in the middle, too wrapped up in their work to be able to concentrate for long on such matters of great principle, there remains one crumb of comfort; whatever development may take place in television, news need have no fear of the future. One sentence from *The Task of Broadcasting News*, a study for the BBC General Advisory Council, says it all:

> "If ever broadcasting were pared to the proverbial bone, news would have to be that bone."[3]

---

[1] *EBU Review*, May, 1975
[2] Robin Day, *Day by Day: A Dose of My Own Hemlock*. (William Kimber, 1975.)
[3] BBC, May, 1976.

GLOSSARY

No glossary can ever hope to be complete or totally satisfy the expert. There are technical terms which are unique to one television service. Some have limited or purely local use. Others have entirely different meanings in different services. The 190-or so definitions listed here are those I have come across personally and are, I believe, among the most widely used and generally accepted.

A

ABC. American Broadcasting Company. American network.

ACMADE. British make of film editing machine.

ACTUALITY. Real. See NATURAL SOUND.

AGENCY TAPE. Written material received on news agency printers.

AMPEX. American make of videotape recording apparatus. Still sometimes used as a generic term for all videotape equipment.

ANCHORMAN/WOMAN. Main presenter of a programme. See also NEWSCASTER, NEWSREADER.

ANIMATION. As used in television news, usually the technique of adding or changing information on a caption *manually*, by means of panels, flaps or tabs which are moved at the appropriate moment during transmission.

AP. Associated Press. American news agency.

ARRIFLEX. West German-made film camera. 16mm sound and silent versions very popular for TV news work.

ASSIGNMENTS EDITOR/MANAGER. Person responsible for assigning reporters and/or film crews/electronic camera units to events for coverage.

ASSIGNMENT SHEET. Written instructions from Assignment editor/manager or other member of news-gathering department, setting out details of an event to be covered.

AUTOCUE. Studio prompting system which enables performers to read from a written script while looking directly to the camera.

B

BBC. British Broadcasting Corporation.

BIRDING. Term for the process of transmitting material by communications satellite. So named after *Early Bird*, the first satellite launched after the creation of Intelsat, the organisation set up to establish a world-wide system.

BP. Back Projection. System for projecting moving or still pictures on to a screen behind a performer in the studio.

BUTT-JOIN. The editing together of two or more films, usually on separate subjects, to create one continuous length of film.

B & W. Black and white.

C

CANS. Earphones.

CAPTION. Generic term for all artwork produced on card or paper.

CAPTION SCANNER (SLIDE CHAIN). Form of fixed electronic camera for transmitting captions. An alternative to photographing them from pin-boards or stands in the studio.

CBS. Columbia Broadcasting System. American network.

CEL. Transparent plastic sheet by which extra information can be added to existing artwork without permanently altering the original. (eg: New locations on a basic map.)

CLEAN FEED. Actuality (natural) sound of an event free from commentary or other added sound.

CONTROL ROOM/GALLERY. Room above or next to the studio, from which production and technical operations are controlled during transmission.

COMMAG. Combined magnetic. System for recording sound on to a magnetic stripe which is bonded to one edge of the film in manufacture. Also known as 'single system' film sound recording.

COMMUNICATIONS SATELLITES. Man-made devices positioned in space as a means of 'bouncing' television or other signals from one part of the globe to another. See INTELSAT.

COPY. Written material for news.

COPY-TASTER. Journalist responsible for the first assessment of all incoming copy, particularly that from agency sources.

CORRESPONDENT. Journalist who is employed to concentrate on a specialist subject or is based in a particular geographical location.

COUNT DOWN. Time count in reverse order, usually spoken aloud in the control room and given by hand-signal in the studio, to ensure the smooth transition from one source to the next. Mostly used in the sequence from ten to zero.

CSO. Colour Separation Overlay. Also known as Chromakey. A means of merging pictures from separate sources electronically, giving the illusion that the performer in the studio is set against a pictorial background. The background is in fact made of a specially chosen plain colour which activates the device.

CUE. Signal given to start or stop action.

CUE DOT. Small circular mark made on an edited film, usually in the top right-hand corner, to indicate that it is coming to an end. Electronic cue dots are usually superimposed in the top left-hand corner of the screen to indicate the approaching end of one programme and to cue in the next.

CUT. (1) An edit (2) A deletion.

CUT-AWAY. Film/videotape editing term for a shot inserted as a means of telescoping the action in a picture sequence while maintaining continuity.

CUT-AWAY QUESTIONS. Those repeated for the camera after an interview to provide a continuity bridge between edited sections.

CUT INS. Extra shots, close-ups for example, which are edited into the main action of a scene.

CUTTING/CLIPPING. Item cut out or copied from a newspaper or other printed reference source.

CUTTING COPY. Copy of a film used for editing purposes.

CUT-OFF. Area of a television picture naturally lost in reaching the domestic screen.

CUTS. Also known as trims or out-takes. The exposed film not included in a cut story (See below).

CUT STORY. Complete and edited news film.

CU. Close-up. Head-and-shoulders shot.

D

DEAF AID. Close-fitting earphone through which a performer in the studio can be given instruction from the control room.

DIARY STORY. News event covered by pre-arrangement.

DOOR-STEPPER. Informal interview obtained after waiting for the subject 'on the door-step.'

DOPE SHEET. Cameraman's detailed record of film shot on location.

DOUBLE CHAIN. System of running two films synchronously on separate telecine machines and switching from one to another to produce an overlay effect.

DOUBLE SYSTEM. (Of recording sound-on-film.) See SEPMAG.

DRY RUN. Rehearsal without the camera.

DUB. To add or re-record sound on to an edited film or videotape recording.

DURATION. Exact length, in time, of a programme or an item within it.

E

EBU. European Broadcasting Union.

EDITOR FOR/OF THE DAY. The senior journalist operationally responsible for all the output of a single television news service on one day.

ENG. Electronic news gathering. Also known as ECC (Electronic camera coverage) or EJ (Electronic journalism). A lightweight electronic camera system for covering news events. Rapidly superseding or supplementing conventional film equipment in the United States and elsewhere.

ESTABLISHING SHOT. Scene-setting shot of people or subject.

EUROVISION. International network for the exchange of television programmes.

EUROVISION NEWS EXCHANGE. System for exchanging news pictures through Eurovision links. At present there are three such exchanges a day, at 1200, 1700 and 1855 Central European Time.

EYELINE. The direction in which the subject is seen to be looking by the camera.

F

FILM BIN. Barrel structure on to which chosen sections of film are hung during editing. It is lined with cloth to prevent damage to the film surface.

FILM LEADER. Portion of blank or numbered film which precedes the first frame of picture. Usually calibrated in seconds to aid count down.

FILM MAKE-UP. The joining of separate films and sound tracks to make up reels of telecine for transmission.

FIRE BRIGADE. Editorial/camera unit assigned at short notice to cover news breaks, usually abroad.

FIXER. Editorial co-ordinator or producer accompanying units in the field. Often acts as the main point of contact between home base and news team on location.

FOGGED. Film spoiled by accidental exposure to light.

FOLLOW-UP. News report based on previously broadcast or published material.

FORMAT. Overall style and 'look' of a programme.

FRAME. A single still picture from a moving film. (25 to the second in British television, 24 in the United States).

FREE PUFF. News item which, by its nature, publicises a product or event.

FX. Sound effects.

G
GALLERY. See CONTROL ROOM.

GRAPHICS. General name for artwork or artwork department.

GUN MIKE. See RIFLE MIKE.

GV. General view.

H
HANDBACK. Performer's form of words used to signal the end of his contribution device.

HAND-CARRIED. Film material or equipment transported personally rather than sent as freight.

HAND-HELD. Camera or other equipment used without a tripod or similar steadying devoice.

HANDOUT. Free publicity material given to a news organisation.

HAND-OVER. Performer's form of words used by a newsreader/presenter, etc. as a cue for another performer. (eg: "Now with the sports news. . . .")

HARD NEWS. 'Straight' news.

HEROGRAM. Effusively worded message of congratulations from base to contributor.

HOT PRESS. Machine for applying selected type faces to caption cards by heat process.

I
INTAKE/INPUT. Department responsible for news-gathering.

INTELSAT. International Telecommunications Satellite Organisation—responsible for the global system by which television news pictures are beamed from one country to others. See COMMUNICATIONS SATELLITES.

INTERVISION. Eastern bloc counterpart of Eurovision.

INJECT. A 'live' contribution to a news programme from a distant source.

ITN. Independent Television News Ltd. Company responsible for providing national news for independent television in Britain.

INTRO. Introduction. Opening sentence of a news story.

INSTANT LETTERING. The sheets of rub-on lettering used in artwork.

J

JOINER. Device for joining separate lengths of film in editing. One common type uses transparent sticky tape, another liquid cement.

JUMP CUT. An edit which destroys pictorial continuity by making a subject appear to jump from one position to another in consecutive shots.

K

KEYING COLOUR. Colour chosen to activate CSO.

KEY LIGHT. Chief source of artificial light for a scene.

KEY SHOT. Master shot of a scene.

L

LAY ON. To arrange coverage.

LEAD. Opening item of a news programme.

LEAD IN. See INTRO.

LEADER. See FILM LEADER.

LIBRARY FILM/VIDEOTAPE. Archive material.

LINE. Telecommunication circuit between transmission and receiving points.

LINE-UP. Period immediately before a recording or transmission during which final technical checks are carried out. ·

LIP SYNC. The exact synchronism of pictures and spoken words as in interviews or pieces to camera.

LIVE. As it is happening.

LOCATION. Geographical position of an event.

LS. Long shot.

M

MAGAZINE. Film container fixed directly to or as integral part of a camera. In news work sound magazines usually contain 16 mm film in 400 ft spools.

MAGAZINE PROGRAMME. Programme which is a mix of 'hard' news and feature items.

MIC/MIKE. Microphone.

MONITOR. Television screen displaying a picture from another source (studio, caption scanner, etc.)

MONOCHROME. Black and white.

MONOPOD. Single extendible pole screwed into the base of a camera to keep it steady during filming.

MULTILATERAL. Shared use by three or more broadcasting services of Eurovision, Communications Satellite or similar links. See also UNILATERAL.

N

NATURAL SOUND (NATSOF). Sound recorded on to film at the same time as the picture.

NBC. National Broadcasting Company. American network.

NECK MIKE. Small lightweight microphone hung on a cord around the neck. Also known as a Personal, or Lavaliere.

NEG. Negative film.

NEWS ORGANISER/EDITOR. Journalist responsible for arranging coverage of news events.

NEWSREADER/NEWSCASTER. Main presenter of a news programme. See also ANCHORMAN/WOMAN.

NEWS-WRITER. Newsroom-based journalist responsible for assembling and writing individual items within a programme.

NODDIES. Reporter's simulated reaction shots for use as cutaways in interviews.

O

OB. Outside broadcast. A transmission from outside a studio. (United States: Remote).

ONION BAG. String bag used for the transport of film. So called for its resemblance to the carriers in which onions are sold.

OOV. Out of Vision. Commentary spoken by unseen reader in the studio during transmission. Also known as 'voice over.'

OUT CUE. The final words of an edited film, videotape recording or studio item.

OUTPUT. Department responsible for the selection and processing of material for transmission.

OUT-TAKES. See CUTS.

OVER CRANK. To run a film camera motor at faster than normal speed (25 frames per second in British television, 24 frames per second in the United States.) When reproduced on a projector running at the correct speed, the action appears to be in slow motion. See also; UNDER CRANK.

OVERLAY. Film/videotape editing technique for matching commentator's recorded soundtrack with relevant pictures.

P

PA. (1) Production assistant. (In BBC TV News the studio director.) (2) Press Association. British national domestic news agency.

PACKAGE. A self-contained news report on film or videotape, usually consisting of a number of different elements.

PAN. Camera movement. On (1) the horizontal plane (pan left to right, pan right to left). On (2) the vertical plane (pan up, pan down.)

PASB. Programme as broadcast. Detailed record of a programme for file purposes. Includes names of staff and outside contributors, interviewees, duration and type of film/videotaped inserts, etc.

PIECE TO CAMERA. Report spoken directly to the camera on location. Also known as stand-upper.

PIGEON. Traveller entrusted with passing film between a camera unit and their base.

POS. Positive. A print from a negative.

PRE-HEAR CUE. The last unwanted portion of sound track (usually speech on VTR) which immediately precedes that which is required. Ensures accuracy in cueing in the desired words at the correct moment on transmission.

PRESENTER. See ANCHORMAN/WOMAN; NEWSREADER/NEWSCASTER.

Q
QUADRUPLEX. Videotape machine with four vision heads recording across a magnetic tape two inches wide.

QUARTER-INCH TAPE. Quarter-inch wide sound recording tape used on conventional reel-to-reel recorders. Widely used in the double system/sepmag method of recording sound on film.

R
RADIO MIKE. Microphone used with small transmitter and therefore needs no cable to connect it with the sound recording equipment of a camera. Effective over relatively long range.

REUTERS. British-based agency supplying foreign news.

REVERSAL FILM. Film type which emerges as a positive after chemical processing. Very popular for news work.

REVERSE PHASE. Electronic means of changing negative to positive for transmission purposes.

RIFLE MIKE. Directional microphone with rifle-shaped barrel.

ROLLER CAPTION (CRAWL). Mechanical device for displaying moving lettering vertically or horizontally across the screen.

ROSTRUM CAMERA. Camera mounted on the photographic enlarger principle to enable static objects to be filmed frame by frame.

ROUGH CUT. First completed assembly of film cut to its approximately pre-selected order and duration.

RUNNING ORDER. Order of transmission of items in a programme.

RUN THROUGH. Rehearsal.

RUN UP. The time considered necessary for technical equipment to reach full operating speed. Usually three seconds for film, ten seconds for VTR.

RUSHES (DAILIES). Exposed and processed film in its unedited form.

S
SCANNER. Mobile control centre serving an outside broadcast unit. (See also CAPTION SCANNER.)

SEPMAG. Separate magnetic system of recording sound on film. The sound is recorded separately on to a tape recorder run in synchronism with the film camera. Also known as sync sound.

SHOT LIST. Detailed written description of each scene in an edited film, from which the words of the commentary can be written to match the pictures. Usually measured in seconds. An essential part of the news-writer's duties.

SINGLE SYSTEM. (Of recording sound on film.) See COMMAG.

SOF. Sound on film.

SOFT. (1) A shot that is slightly out of focus. (2) A news item considered interesting rather than important.

SOUND TRACK. The film or tape on to which sound is recorded.

SOUP. Processing plant for film.

SPARKS. Electrician or lighting assistant.

SPLIT SCREEN. A picture composed of two separate elements, each occupying half of the screen area.

STEENBECK. West German-made film editing machine.

STICK MIKE. Stick-shaped microphone much used in news work for its speed of preparation.

STILL. A single picture.

STILL FRAME. A single picture from a moving film stopped on its way through Telecine (See below).

STOCK. Raw unused film.

STRINGER. A freelance contributor employed on a regular basis.

STRIPE. The narrow band of magnetic sound track used in the commag/single system of recording sound on film.

STUDIO SPOT. (1) A contribution made in the studio during transmission by a performer other than the main presenter of a programme. Or (2) any form of studio item involving two or more participants. (eg: an interview.)

SUPERIMPOSITION. Usually abbreviated to super. Electronic or optical combination of two or more pictures to give extra information on the screen. (eg. The addition of a speaker's name or title during an interview.)

T

TALK-BACK. One-way sound link between control room and other technical areas.

TALKING HEAD. Any interviewee. Also pejorative: to have too many talking heads in a programme is considered unimaginative.

TELECINE. Projector/TV camera mechanism for transmitting film on television. Usually abbreviated to TC. BBC term is TK: their abbreviation TC stands for Television Centre, headquarters of the BBC Television Service.

TELEPROMPTER. Studio prompting device. See AUTOCUE.

TELE-RECORDING. Process of recording programmes or items by filming them off high-quality monitors. The film has to be chemically processed in the conventional way.

TILT. A vertical panning movement of the camera.

TRIPOD. Adjustable three-legged stand fixed to the base of a camera to keep it steady during filming.

TWO SHOT. A shot of two people.

TX. Transmission.

U

UNDER CRANK. To run a film camera motor at slower than normal speed (25 frames per second in British television, 24 frames per second in the United States.) When reproduced on a projector running at the correct speed the action appears faster than normal. See also OVER CRANK.

UNILATERAL. Exclusive use by one broadcasting organisation of Eurovision, communications satellite or similar links.

UPITN. International newsfilm agency part-owned by ITN.

UPCUT. American term for the accidental overlapping of two sound sources (eg: live commentary running into recorded sound.)

205

V

VIDEOTAPE RECORDER/(VT/VTR). Machine for recording sound and pictures electronically for instant reproduction. See also AMPEX.

VISION STORY. BBC term for an item or part of an item read by the newsreader without further illustration.

VISNEWS. International newsfilm agency part-owned by the BBC.

VOICE OVER. See OOV.

VOX POP. Vox Populi. A series of very short interviews on a specific topic, usually with people selected at random, and edited together to give a cross-section of public opinion.

W

WHIP PAN (ZIP PAN). Very high speed panning movement of the camera.

WILD TRACK/WILD SOUND. Recorded sound which is related to but not synchronised with the picture.

WIPE. (1) A production technique: the method of progressively displacing one picture electronically to reveal another. (2) To erase a recording.

Z

ZOOM LENS. A lens giving a variable focal length.

FURTHER READING

A History of Broadcasting in the United States, by Erik Barnouw
three vols. (Oxford University Press, 1966–70).

A Survey of Television, by Stuart Hood (Heinemann, 1967).

BBC Handbooks, published annually (BBC Publications).

Broadcasting in Britain, 1922–1972, by Keith Geddes (HMSO,
1972).

Day by Day: a Dose of My Own Hemlock, by Robin Day (William
Kimber, 1975).

Effective TV Production, by Gerald Millerson (Focal Press 1976).

Factual Television, by Norman Swallow (Focal Press, 1966).

Here is the News, by Richard Baker (Leslie Frewin, 1966).

In and Out of the Box, by Robert Dougall (Collins/Harvill 1973).

Prime Time: the Life of Edward R. Murrow, by Alexander
Kendrick (Dent & Sons, 1970).

Radio and Television, by Stuart Hood (David & Charles, 1975).

Report of the Committee on the Future of Broadcasting (Chairman
Lord Annan) (HMSO, London, 1977).

Reuters' Century, 1851–1951, by Graham Storey (Max Parrish,
1951).

Sound and Fury, by Maurice Gorham (Percival Marshall, 1948).

Television, A Personal Report, by Robin Day (Hutchinson, 1961).

Television Graphics, by Ron Hurrell (Thames & Hudson, 1972).

Television News, by Richard Collins (British Film Institute
Television Monograph, 1976).

Television News Reporting, by CBS News (McGraw-Hill, 1958).

Television Newsfilm Techniques, by Vernon Stone and Bruce
Hinson (Hastings House, 1974).

Television and Radio News, by Bob Siller, Ted White and Hal
Terkel (MacMillan, 1960).

Television/Radio News Workbook, by Irving Fang, Ph.D (Hastings
House, New York, 1975).

Ten Seconds From Now, by Godfrey Talbot (Hutchinson, 1973).

The EBU Review, The TV News Exchange, May, 1975.

The History of Broadcasting in the United Kingdom, by Asa Briggs 3 vols. 4th vol. in prep. (Oxford University Press, 1961–70).

The Least Worst Television in the World, by Milton Shulman (Barrie & Jenkins, 1973).

The Mirror in the Corner, by Peter Black (Hutchinson, 1972).

The New Priesthood, by Joan Bakewell and Nicholas Garnham (Allen Lane, Penguin Press, 1973).

The Ravenous Eye, by Milton Shulman (Collins, 1973).

The Shadow in the Cave, by Anthony Smith (Allen & Unwin, 1973).

The Task of Broadcasting News, a study for the BBC General Advisory Council (BBC, 1976).

The Technique of Television Announcing, by Bruce Lewis (Focal Press, 1966).

The Universal Eye. World Television in the Seventies, by Timothy Green (The Bodley Head, 1972).

The Work of the Television Journalist, by Robert Tyrrell (Focal Press, 1972).

Today and Yesterday, by John Timpson (George Allen & Unwin, 1976).

To Kill a Messenger. Television News and the Real World, by William Small (Hastings House, 1970).

Workers in World News, by Bernard Moore (Pergamon Press).

INDEX

212

214